THE RISE OF THE OVERCOMER

High Gate Press, LLC
2145B Hoffmeyer Rd.
Florence, SC 29501
www.highgatepress.com

ISBN: 978-0-9904625-5-2
Graphics and Layout by Sarah Fender
Cover by Mehreen Shaukat and Candy Smith

DEDICATION

This book is dedicated to my husband, James, and my children: Traclyn, Raven, Jamyn, Shira-Sion, and Justice. Each of you is my inspiration to become more. For this reason, I will always live to demonstrate the truth of God, which is my God-created identity as an overcomer.

This book is also dedicated to my mother, Sheila Green, my grandmother, Rita Mae Ridgley, and my aunt, Debra Franklin Jefferson. Their humility, strength, and determination, along with true love for God and people, positioned all their descendants to walk in a cycle of blessing.

I know what it means to lack, and I know what it means to experience overwhelming abundance. For I'm trained in the secret of overcoming all things, whether in fullness or in hunger. And I find that the strength of Christ's explosive power infuses me to conquer every difficulty.

— Philippians 4:12-13 TPT

TABLE OF CONTENTS

The Lie
Types of Fear
Our Deepest Fear
Defeat Fear

Take Your Seat
Show Up—What Satan Fears Most
Victory over the Lies of Fear

The Effects of Pain
Hurt and the Cycle of Control
Process Pain in the Right Way
Apply the Word to Pain
Overcoming Church Hurt
Action To Overcome Hurt

Pride That Binds the Mind
Pride and Our Thinking
Harmful Cycles of Pride
Overcoming Pride of Criticism and Judgment
Overcoming Religious Pride
God's Thoughts and Wisdom Above Our Thoughts
Pride Solutions
Father Knows Best

Religion

FOREWORD

Very few times have I picked up a book and not laid it down until I read it from beginning to end. I did this with Robyn F. Vincent's *The Rise of the Overcomer: Possessing the Power To Go Beyond and Triumph.* This book helps us process warfare and the faith necessary to live in an overcoming dimension.

When we receive revelation from God, we need to engage in warfare against the enemy to see God's purposes established. God calls us to fight the good fight. We don't settle for the status quo. We don't accept passivity. We stand on God's revelation, and we *battle* in prayer. We allow God to produce warfare faith within us. As we press through in faith we overcome.

Stay in the battle until the breakthrough comes. Allow God to produce overcoming faith in you! The result of overcoming faith is that the glory of God is manifested in your midst. God has called you to enter the fullness of His promises. He has called you to live in His glory. Clothe yourself in manifested, or glory, faith.

Ask yourself, *What dimension of faith am I presently walking in?* Then ask God what you need to do to enter a new dimension. Wherever you are, keep moving forward!

God has called you to win your battles. A victor's crown awaits those who will overcome. You can overcome the enemy and gain the victory!

Robyn has given us a roadmap to help us keep moving toward our overcoming destination. The truth of the matter is that we will overcome! Revelation 12:10-12 says,

> *Then I heard a loud voice saying in heaven, "Now salvation, and strength, and the kingdom of our God,*

and the power of His Christ have come, for the accuser of our brethren, who accused them before our God day and night, has been cast down. And they overcame him by the blood of the Lamb and by the word of their testimony, and they did not love their lives to the death. Therefore rejoice, O heavens, and you who dwell in them! Woe to the inhabitants of the earth and the sea! For the devil has come down to you, having great wrath, because he knows that he has a short time."

Daniel 11:32 adds, "Those who do wickedly against the covenant he shall corrupt with flattery; but the people who know their God shall be strong, and carry out *great exploits.*" Our future may be filled with conflict, but the Lord has developed an overcoming anointing in us. I define overcoming like this: We are able to receive a supernatural power or strength to conquer or defeat anything that is distressing us or attempting to stop us from advancing on our path. We all want to advance on our path, not only as individuals but also as a corporate body.

Here are six things that I see summarized in this book:

1. We must understand authority.

Authority is the key to power. No greater faith had Jesus seen in all Israel than that of the man who understood authority (see Matt. 8:5-13). The Lord showed me that if I would begin to understand and analyze every authority that had influence in my life, I would begin to operate in a new level of faith. To the extent that we submit to the authority God has placed in our lives, our faith has the opportunity to be stretched and strengthened. Faith is the overcoming agent that God's people have on this earth (see John 14:12); therefore, if the church is to overcome, we must understand and submit to proper authority.

2. We must deal with our greatest fears.

The spirit of fear creates an unsound mind, weakens power, and negates love. The Lord showed me that, at the end of each ten-year period, a new move of holiness will begin to emerge among His people that will unleash a genuine fear of the Lord. He also showed me that a new administrative move of God has to come into each time frame.

The fear of the Lord releases wisdom, and wisdom will unlock and dismantle demonic forces. They are a structured hierarchy that forms a government, and governments have to be dismantled. We cannot shout down principalities and powers. Wisdom causes false governments to topple. If we will tear down the spirit of fear that is hindering us and move into a new fear of the Lord, we will topple iniquitous patterns that allow principalities and powers to blind unreached people groups, cities, and even entire nations to the light of the gospel.

3. We must increase our discernment.

Every time I have received a vision of the future, the Lord has also spoken words that have given me courage. "But Lord, I do not have the ability to discern at this level," I have often said. And each time, it was as if the Lord said I did not have a choice. *Discipline yourself in the Word and exercise My Spirit within your spirit*, He said, *for it will take both Word and Spirit to cause the reality of Me to be seen in days ahead*. If we quench the Holy Spirit in our lives, or if we do not wash ourselves with the written Word, we fall out of spiritual balance and open ourselves to delusion. Under those conditions we can never reach the level of discernment we will need for the critical times ahead.

4. We must know who labors among us and who comes into our sphere of authority.

The Lord has blessed me with an incredible team of watchmen

who keep the post at the door to see who comes in and out, what they are bringing in, and what they are attempting to receive once they come into my sphere of authority. Without these faithful men and women, our sphere could be penetrated by adverse forces trying to lead us astray.

It is imperative that God's people communicate necessary information to one another efficiently during these times. The Lord showed me that He is going to start building true unity of purpose and function within His body from territory to territory. I began to see a network that will form a net. When this net is completed, He will begin to drag it through cities and nations, collecting a great harvest. I saw that everyone in the regional body will need to be connected to each other, with everyone working to accomplish God's purposes for that territory. One reason we will need to know each other and be linked together is to help discern when infiltrators attempt to undermine God's purposes.

5. We must not allow the world to conform us to its blueprint. However, we must not fear the world either. The prince of the power of the air rules this earth. Satan loves to find places in our human nature where he can ensnare us to do his will. To prevent this, Christians often distance themselves from the world. They become separatists, and the root of their actions is fear and religious pride.

When we get cleaned up, we are always a little afraid that the temptations of this world will get us dirty once again. But we are to be like Jesus: in the world but not "of this world" (John 8:23). The Lord is planning for the glory that He is about to release in His church to permeate the Earth. We cannot spread His glory if we hide out.

6. We must understand the wealth of the kingdom that is being prepared for the righteous.

God is planning a great transference of wealth to His people. Wealth does not just mean having money but also having strength and the spoils of war (in this case, a harvest of souls). I believe God wants us to understand money and finances so we will be good stewards to advance His kingdom in the future. If we allow God to purify us and make us holy, He will then be able to trust us with great wealth.

In *The Rise of the Overcomer*, Robyn fully displays that the Lord is on our side. This book will help develop a new strength, a new faith, and a new glory experience with each page that is read. We are an awesome army that cannot be stopped as we go forth.

Sin will have no authority over you! Evil will not be able to reign in your atmosphere. Troubles will not overwhelm you when you are walking with an overcoming strength in your spirit. As you read *The Rise of the Overcomer*, you will experience this very thing happening within your inner being.

Dr. Chuck D. Pierce
President of Glory of Zion International and
Kingdom Harvest Alliance

ACKNOWLEDGEMENTS

First and foremost, all praises and thanks to God Almighty for His faithfulness, wisdom, vision, and perfecting grace that led me to complete this book and its journey successfully. Without Him, this would have never been possible.

I would like to express my deep and sincere gratitude to my leader Dr. Chuck Pierce for believing in me and supporting that which I am called and created to do. His wisdom, guidance, and pioneering spirit have deeply inspired me to always look beyond the norm, believe for greater possibilities, press past the turmoil, and become the change agent needed in chaos. Building buildings is one thing, but building people is another. His teachings, contributions, impartations, and mentorship have taught me the importance and value of building up people. I am honored to serve at the Global Spheres Center under his leadership.

I would like to boastfully express immense gratitude for my beautiful parents, the late Nelson Franklin and Sheila Green, whose pure hearts were completely unmatched. Their unfailing love, support, and sacrifice gave me an opportunity that they were never able to access. I deeply honor the commitment they made to ensure that their children knew they could accomplish anything as long as they courageously occupied their space in this world.

I also want to thank and honor the gifted women God has used in more ways than I could ever count to propel me forward and keep me centered on the path of destiny. Pamela Pierce, Melinda Richardson, Janice Swinney, Toni Hatfield, Anne Tate, and Linda Heidler are women of distinct honor in my life. Their wisdom, knowledge, prayers, and generosity have truly been transformational. Their words of encouragement pushed me forward and propelled me to stand confidently in my God-given identity and to unashamedly manifest it wherever I go.

A huge debt of gratitude goes out to Ann Lovett for helping me through the writing process. She assisted me in the editing and helped me to develop the framework that God destined for me to complete.

Last but certainly not least, I give a very sincere thanks to all others who supported me throughout this process. Many will come into the knowledge and truth of God's loving plan for them because of you.

INTRODUCTION

In the book of Revelation, God repeatedly pronounces blessings upon the one who overcomes. It is the message of God that hangs over a generation like a signpost. It is the banner and standard that all human souls will be judged by when they stand before their Maker. How we press towards the finish line, how we endure the fight, or how we handle the task at hand and steward the assignments are all aspects of life that show the true measure of faith we have to overcome. The Eternal One, God our Father, is cheering us on and daily making provision to ensure that we His children overcome every obstacle or adversary to gain the prize of our high calling. We must apprehend those things which He bestows upon us to seize the fullness of life and liberty we've been given.

A while back, on just an ordinary day, I had a very captivating and sobering experience while reading the book of Revelation. That event opened my eyes to see my journey differently and led me to leave behind a familiar, mediocre, routinized, superficial way of life. At the same time, it propelled me into a new life of undistracted devotion and freedom to become a person I was not familiar with—the person whom God had made me to be. I could see the enormous amount of love that God has for us, and that's what inspired me to write this book.

This is what I desire for you. I want you to experience a new journey and to encounter God differently until every part of your spirit is made alive and free, no longer being tossed to and fro or feeling subject to the tumultuous waves of circumstance and culture.

God desires for us to see more than what we presently see, to perceive those things which keep us from blessings, peace, purpose, and prosperity. He wants us all to know what causes us to stumble, so that we are always able to overcome. From the depths of His heart, the Lord wants each of us to experience the power of His love. He wants us to get used to being seated in heavenly places and ruling with Him from His throne room.

And he who overcomes, and keeps My works until the end, to him I will give power over the nations.

— Revelation 2:26

It's not easy but it's doable. It starts with the depth of His love. Love is the key to overcoming all things. Love deals with stewardship, respect, honor, multiplication, and promotion. The Bible tells us that love is the greatest gift of all (see 1 Cor. 13:13). It surpasses all things. The Word of God descriptively reads that God Himself is love (see 1 Jn. 4:8). I am one who is deeply marked and transformed by that radical, fiery love, so I wanted to make this book as practical and attainable as I possibly could.

I decided to share these revelations because I witnessed the transformation in others as I explained these truths through workshops, mentorship, and teachings. I saw amazing transformation and increase in their lives by simply equipping them to understand the depths of God's rich, powerful love and what it does in the lives of people who give room for it. People came into my life one way and left a completely different way. They progressed by leaps and bounds.

It is important to me that you receive the guidance, wisdom, and instruction you need to succeed in your divine calling and to live a life of triumph. As you read this book, I pray you will gain the understanding and clarity to live an overcoming life. My prayer is that you receive the strength, grace, and vision to accomplish anything the Lord calls you to do in this new era.

2

In Proverbs 4, God tells us to get understanding:

Wisdom is *the principal thing;*
Therefore *get wisdom.*
And in all your getting, get understanding.

— *Proverbs 4:7*

I endeavor to give you insight and understanding for a victorious way of living. This book will set new courses and write new chapters in your life, which will produce a greater storyline that can only be written by the Author of all creation, not just for you but also for the generations coming behind you.

Everyone ultimately desires to see healthy transformation happening around us so we can flourish and possess the most fruitful and favorable outcome. This is also the original intent of the Lord for each of us, before man was ever formed. This is the life He dreamed of and made possible for those who would come to Him. Now it is time to open our eyes and allow God to lift us up so that we can begin the journey to discover the people we are truly meant to be at this historical moment.

CHAPTER 1
LET LOVE ARISE

When I became a new believer in Christ, the world around me drastically changed. Everything I knew seemed to be exposed for what it truly was. For the first time in my life, it felt like I could see "behind the curtain." Things and people who had made me feel happy at one time now seemed to leave me feeling drained and empty. That was a tremendous game changer for me. The things I normally ran to now dissatisfied me because my soul was longing for a touch from God every moment of every hour of every day.

When we have a true encounter with God, it marks us for life. We can try to go back to normal life or business as usual, but it seems like we are just spinning our wheels. The presence of God can never be removed. Once we've seen Him, we can't unsee Him. Once we've experienced Him, we can't act like we haven't. Oddly, we are different but still the same person.

That's where I was. I couldn't understand how to be this new creature in Christ, but I also knew that I couldn't hold on to my dark thoughts and remain in a way of life that left me feeling empty and worthless. During that time, it was hard to understand where I was in life and how I was supposed to move forward.

When I went to church, I'd hear words such as faith, prayer, and grace over and over again. I did not really understand these concepts because they were not a part of my everyday vocabulary. This left me feeling inadequate because I was fully aware of my frail humanity every time I was immersed in praise and worship. Whenever I exalted Him, the greatness of who He is became greatly magnified, while the need for Him increased in my heart. When I saw my sinful thoughts and attitudes, I would ask Jesus to change me. Sometimes it was easy and sometimes it was gut-wrenching because I knew I had to allow Him to work His truth in me and cover me in a new way. He had to peel away all the layers of lies that for years I had used to cover my flaws and insecurities. No matter how messy my situation looked, the Lord was always full of compassion as He spoke to my wounded soul.

Not long after I committed my life to God, I was speaking to Him, trying to be as honest as I could. I said, "Lord, teach me how to pray. I really don't know how to, but of course, you know that already, right?"

He responded and said, *Robyn, pray this prayer to Me every day and I'll do the rest. Say these words, "Lord, let me love You more, and don't let me be deceived."*

I felt like that was way too simple. Besides, I didn't feel that I loved Him or had the capacity to love Him at that moment. As a result, I felt like I was a bit of a hypocrite, and I hated being a hypocrite! But I still obeyed because He was already proving himself to be trustworthy to me, even in the early days of our relationship. He performed many extraordinary miracles for me and my kids during those times, so why would I doubt His words?

So I did it. I did it out of obedience. I prayed that simple prayer for weeks, and then weeks turned into years. He caused my heart to enlarge and be filled with a greater capacity to love. Without me even being aware of it, I had developed a sincere and deep love for God and others. It was completely supernatural.

My behaviors and desires drastically altered. I began to yearn for His presence in the middle of my workday. I would listen to worship music at work just to feel a deeper connection to the Lord. What? This was not my norm. I can't even repeat some of the songs I used to listen to before I committed my heart to

Christ. Seriously!

Through this experience, God began to let me know that our relationship was based on His work, not mine. He allowed me to know that it was by His Spirit that I was drawn to Him, redeemed by Him, and now walking in communion with Him. I did not initiate any of it. As a matter of fact, the Lord spoke all these things to me before I knew any of them were written in the Bible.

LOVE IS EVERYTHING

"Lord, let me love You more," was a prayer that God began to form within my heart. He aligned my heart with the words that I was speaking by faith, and He made my confession true. My heart began to deeply desire to love Him with all my being. It was like a divine exchange happening. When I spoke those words to God, He went to work and caused them to materialize within me! I did not realize this process was occurring at the time. As a matter of fact, it was months later when I realized that it was no longer hard to pray or cry out to the Lord. I was no longer second-guessing myself, wondering if I was speaking the right words or saying the right prayers. I was boldly expressing my feelings and thoughts because I had developed a beautiful relationship with Him. My heart was overflowing with love and passion for God, and all I wanted was more of Him in every moment of the day. I had become a brand new person!

Church was no longer a chore for me, like it had been when I was growing up. It became a place where I went to meet with God. Whenever I showed up there, I knew that He would be waiting to meet me. I was filled with much excitement and anticipation, and I knew that every experience would be better than the last one. It was as if life was being infused into me. I came alive! I was no longer confused and disappointed. I was filled with hope again. Even my speech completely changed. It was wild. I was believing for better things and greater outcomes, not just for myself but also for everyone around me.

Praying the simple prayer that God had spoken to my heart caused me to develop a genuine relationship with Him, and this changed everything. I received so much more than I could give. It's funny to consider how I initially felt shameful and embarrassed over my lack of spiritual depth. But God already knew that the only thing I could give Him was my heart, and that's exactly what He wanted. It was my lustful desires, hidden motives, and wrong intentions that needed to change so I could see all that He had for me. Please hear me: Those things weren't going to change until I received something greater that revealed the truth about me and my heart's true condition. With love, God exposed me, but then He covered me. He revealed my insecurities and gave me more grace to overcome. I felt like Abraham in Genesis 15. God spoke to Abraham concerning his fear so He could reassure him of His unending provision and protection.

> *After these things the word of the LORD came to Abram in a vision, saying, "Do not be afraid, Abram. I am your shield, your exceedingly great reward."*

> — *Genesis 15:1*

GOD'S LOVE OVERCOMES

I experienced a lot of inner healing and deliverance during my first few years as a Christian. God filled me with His loving Spirit and made me into a brand new person who could overcome anything. The more I encountered God's love, the more layers of filth were washed away from me. Everything from fear and insecurity to fornication, manipulation, and drunkenness. I was literally transformed by the power of God's mercy, goodness, and love. This intimate relationship was so pure and full of light that it broke off every form of darkness that had once strongly oppressed and held me captive. I was so free I could hardly keep it to myself!

God's love sets us free from all those things that hold us back and attempt to confine us. So when I prayed, "Lord let me love You more, and don't let me be deceived," it was liberating me from everything that had kept me bound!

As long as my desires were directed toward all the wrong people and places, I could never seem to produce anything good in my life. My fallacies caused me to live in a pit of falsehood, foolery, and fantasy. But God stepped in and transformed everything for me. He was beyond merciful. He was beyond forgiving. He became my everything.

That's how much God fervently loves us. He wants to demonstrate that love in many different ways, so that we can see it with our own eyes and willingly embrace it. Because He is so deeply committed and invested, He will mercifully fill our mouths with the right words, give us the right heart, and lead us onto the right course so that we can know Him and experience life in a fuller way. He completely flips the script and changes the entire narrative from absolutely nothing to an extraordinary something. Incredible!

When we allow the power of love to flood our hearts, we gain faith and peace over our future. It shifts the old, tainted mindsets that hold us back from the blessings we were meant to obtain. God breaks those chains off our hearts so that we are free to worship, love, and follow His leading. We come alive and enter a new dimension where we are truly able to experience the blessing of covenant. He takes us by the hand and leads us into His predestined, covenant plan.

The Lord operates through covenant relationships. It's through these committed relationships that He sovereignly establishes His purposes and promises for His children. We must learn to faithfully walk with Him to see His plan revealed.

For instance, let's look at Joshua's life, which is a great testimony of this. In the first chapter of the book of Joshua, God told him that Moses was dead, and now the time had come for him to arise and lead the people of Israel into the land where His promises would be fulfilled. However, if he was going to be successful, he would have to meditate on God's instructions day and night so the order of God could be established and the Israelites could be victorious.

The Hebrew word *hagah*, which means *meditate*, denotes the action of speaking and pondering. So, God spoke and told Joshua to speak and ponder His words day and night. This would establish his success as a leader and cause the nation of Israel to possess the land that God had promised to all the descendants of Abraham.

I believe it is vitally important for each of us to understand and remember two major facts. First and foremost, God chooses us. Secondly, it's God's predetermined plan that we are fulfilling, not our own. Although we get to enjoy many benefits from following God, we must remember that we are here to carry out our divine mandate. We cannot pursue blessings, benefits, or other material, superficial things and expect to fulfill divine destiny. God's plan is bigger than our individual purpose. The only way to establish the Master's plan is to follow the original blueprint and execute it according to how the Master sees fit. Remember, the pure in heart see God. Everything is fulfilled through love, and God will fulfill every promise because He loves us.

FOLLOW THE LEADER

I know what's going on in your head right now. You're asking yourself, "Could it possibly be that easy?" Well, the answer is both yes and no. Yes, because we can simply follow God's instructions. And no, because we must be able to see God and how He's moving. We must know the divine wisdom or revelation that He's presenting so we can overcome every hindrance, temptation, or stumbling block that would prevent us from successfully fulfilling our purpose in the earth. Revealed knowledge is the key that causes us to walk on the path that God has for us.

> *Your word* is *a lamp to guide my feet and a light to my path.*
>
> — *Psalm 119:105 NLT*

> *The commandments of the LORD are right, bringing joy to the heart. The commands of the LORD are clear, giving insight for living.*
>
> — *Psalm 19:8 NLT*

We don't have to strive to get into a new season or to fulfill God's purpose. All we must do is seek Him. God fulfills every one of His promises because He deeply loves us. He does not expect or need us to be perfect. There's room for error in our relationship with Him. His Spirit will lead, perfect, and position us so that we receive everything we need. God doesn't want us to continue to crash and burn every time we get a second wind. He wants us to come alive and thrive. He wants us to advance with supernatural strength and favor, just as He planned. He sees us taking giant leaps of faith, breaking through the most difficult situations, and passionately changing the world because God himself lives on the inside of us.

So make a decision today to cease striving and allow Him to show you the path, the obstacles, and the keys that you need to manifest everything you're meant to be! Proverbs declares of man,

As he thinks in his heart, so is *he . . .*

— *Proverbs 23:7*

The Hebrew word for *think* symbolizes or represents a gatekeeper. A gatekeeper grants or forbids access to something, some place, or someone. So this passage states that how a person keeps watch over their own heart is directly correlated to how that person will exist or live. For this reason, it's important for us to be honest, humble, and discerning. These things will cause us to receive and understand our world very differently from how we perceive it at this moment.

Before you read the rest of this book, make yourself a promise right now and say, "I am becoming a person who is bold and full of faith, actively pursuing God to establish true purpose and apprehend victory in every area of life. I will leave no stone unturned and will yield myself fully to God's higher plan. This is the hour that I will rise and overcome!"

Now let's go!

MEDITATION FOR APPLICATION

Set aside 15-30 minutes each day to commune with God. Each day read and meditate on one of the Scriptures listed below. Follow these steps.

1. Get in a quiet place without distraction.

2. Play a praise song and just listen to the words.

3. Ask God to reveal His heart and meaning to you as you read the Scriptures.

4. Write your reflections below or in your journal.

5. Read the Scriptures daily so you receive maximum revelation.

Psalm 119:105 NKJV
Psalm 19:8 NLT
Proverbs 23:7 NKJV
Genesis 5:1 NKJV

MOMENTS OF REFLECTION

1. How did meditating on God's Word impact your attitude and actions?

2. Describe a time in the last week when God's love flowed over you and helped you see clearly in a situation.

3. Notice your thought life over the next week. How are your thoughts impacting your perspective on the world and your joy?

4. Is God your everything? Start to tell Him that in everything, in every situation. Notice how your heart and mind change.

Notes:

CHAPTER 2
SEE YOUR WAY OUT

What delight comes to the one who follows God's
ways!
He won't walk in step with the wicked,
nor share the sinner's way,
nor be found sitting in the scorner's seat.
His passion is to remain true to the Word of "I AM,"
meditating day and night on the true revelation of
light.
He will be standing firm like a flourishing tree
planted by God's design,
deeply rooted by the brooks of bliss,
bearing fruit in every season of life.
He is never dry, never fainting,
ever blessed, ever prosperous.

— *Psalm 1:1-3 TPT*

When God pours love into our hearts, it affects every part of us. It's like a torrential downpour that will not stop until everything is saturated and transformed by the rain of heaven. Our mindsets, thoughts, appetites, and desires begin to go through a drastic change as the soil of our heart softens.

Allow me to paint another picture. When Love Himself is infusing our human heart, it's like having some sort of medical procedure done that we can't undo. It causes us to see and do things differently, shifting our very existence into a brand-new way of life. We can't eat the same, drink the same, or enjoy the same company of people. A deep work goes on inside of us to make room for new plantings that will produce new fruit. This rich, uncommon love does not come to make our lives easier; it comes to make our lives better and much more fruitful.

Every single one of us has a unique destiny and purpose. We discover it by allowing ourselves to become enlightened in new ways. God has a thousand ways to give us what we need, but we must be willing to receive it however He sends it. Many times, we miss these divine parcels that God sends because we resist the one who is delivering them. However, the one who delivers is not actually the sender. The Lord is the sender, as stated in James 1.

Every good gift and every perfect gift is from above, and comes down from the Father of lights, with whom there is no variation or shadow of turning.

— James 1:17

So, if it is a gift that will help us remain rooted in God and cause us to grow, multiply, and be successful, it is sent from the God of Love. When God sends us these different expressions of His lovingkindness, we increase and flourish beyond our wildest dreams. It opens new doors and dimensions that we have yet to dream about. So what are some of these expressions that we need to apprehend if we're truly going to overcome?

Let's take a deeper look at the different facets of love. Wise counsel is an expression of love. Faith is an expression of love. Peace is an expression of love. Joy is an expression of love. Service expresses honor and love. Promotion is an expression of love. Justice expresses bold love. Courage expresses brave love. Even vision, truth, and purpose work by love.

Are you seeing this? Growth and prosperity are rooted in love. Growth comes from loving correction and instruction. As we grow, we develop, increase, and multiply. Prosperity is the fruit of a willingness to grow and be taught. For this reason, we should never be unwilling to learn or receive correction because it is directly connected to our level of growth and prosperity.

Healing, strength, confidence, and wholeness are also rooted in love. Whether we receive healing through natural or supernatural means, God gives it because of His grace and consideration for us. His healing power is activated by persistent, attentive, nonjudgmental support and compassion. Once a person experiences this type of love repeatedly, new patterns of healing are established, which cause the heart and soul to enter a greater measure of inner peace, strength, and confidence. At this point we begin to feel whole and become who we were meant to be all along. Wholeness brings forth a strong, confident sense of identity. We experience a regeneration that affects us mentally, emotionally, physically, and even relationally. It feels like we have been made new!

For this reason, we must understand this truth. All of life flows from the place of love. God is love and there is no greater reality of love and life outside of Him. If we receive the expressions of love that He gives, we will possess the life that He promises. Anything that challenges this truth causes us to forfeit the life we were meant to live. So we must discipline ourselves to live by the truth that is found in God alone. Then we'll experience the joy and riches of our covenant that only His words can bring.

Are you ready to go deeper? Okay, let's put on our goggles and dive in.

LIFE OUTSIDE OF LOVE

When we look at the first chapter of Genesis, we learn that within a few days God meticulously created the universe and everything in it. He was intentional, calculated, and determined to establish this beautiful plan of His so that He could have fellowship and communion with God-like beings on Earth. But look at the sequence of events. He created day and night, land and seas, plants and animals, and every other living thing. Then He created a man called Adam and a woman named Eve. As a side note, this means these things were created for mankind and not mankind created for things.

> *Then God blessed them and said, "Be fruitful and multiply. Fill the earth and govern it. Reign over the fish in the sea, the birds in the sky, and all the animals that scurry along the ground." Then God said, "Look! I have given you every seed-bearing plant throughout the earth and all the fruit trees for your food. And I have given every green plant as food for all the wild animals, the birds in the sky, and the small animals that scurry along the ground— everything that has life." And that is what happened. Then God looked over all he had made, and he saw that it was very good!*
>
> *— Genesis 1:28-31 NLT*

God blessed them and gave them the ability to prosper in every way. He gave them authority and dominion over everything on the earth. He told them to multiply and fill the earth because every form of provision had been made. They could literally eat, rule, and be merry.

Can you imagine that? However, we know the story in Genesis 3 and exactly what happened next. After God blessed Adam, He lovingly gave him instructions that were supposed to keep him from falling into sinful temptation or becoming a

18

lesser version of the glorious being God had created. He told Adam not to eat the fruit of the tree of the knowledge of good and evil, for if he did, he would experience death. Later Eve, Adam's newly created wife, fell prey to the cunningness of the serpent. That crafty, evil serpent convinced her to do the very thing that God had instructed them not to do. Then she offered the fruit from the tree of knowledge to Adam, and he partook of the fruit along with His wife.

So here's the question: What changed to cause their fall? Was it their environment or their situation? Was it the amount of provision? Did God change His mind? Were their privileges and power revoked? Did their physical bodies suddenly give out on them? No, it was their way of seeing. Their seeing changed, and they received a lie. That lie altered the truth of God's Word and led them to a destructive alternative.

When the enemy convinced them that God had not disclosed the truth, they received the lie of their adversary, the devil. This caused deception to enter into the equation of life. The enemy tainted the words of God, and they began to believe and perceive wrongly. They were no longer able to see the abundant, extravagant life that God had provided for them. All they could see was the one tree that existed outside of the boundaries of God's love.

The third chapter of Genesis tells us exactly what happened after they disobeyed the instruction of the Lord. It says,

> *Then the eyes of both of them were opened, and they knew that they were naked; and they sewed fig leaves together and made themselves coverings.*

> — *Genesis 3:7*

Now, once again, let's ask the obvious question: What eyes

were opened? Their physical eyes were still intact because we read that Eve first saw the fruit and then desired it. So what set of eyes were now opened? Evil eyes were activated within their souls when they communed with the cunning serpent and ate of the evil, forbidden tree. The eyes of their understanding could no longer see the perfection of God; they could only see the imperfections and flaws of creation. Guilt and shame caused them to hide and protect themselves from God.

Let's stop right here and take a moment to notice what was not happening. Let's look through the eyes of God to gain clear understanding. We must understand and recognize the value of God's love and grace in moments like this when we fall short and disobey Him. Father God will continue to extend love, no matter how much we mess things up. He does not change. However, would the storyline have changed if they had confessed their sin and asked for forgiveness? Probably, based on what we see in Psalms 51 and 34.

> *You will not reject a broken and repentant heart,*
> *O God.*
>
> — *Psalm 51:17 NLT*

> *The LORD is near to those who have a broken heart,*
> *And saves such as have a contrite spirit.*
>
> — *Psalm 34:18*

So this is how we know that repentance would have definitely helped their situation turn for the better. Hearts of repentance would have opened their eyes and moved them beyond their shame. The Lord would have gladly come to their rescue and turned them back to His truth. This simple act of confession would have caused them to remain in God's presence and live a life of perpetual blessing.

When we don't see ourselves or others as the beautifully created plantings of the Lord, we must understand that we're viewing them, and ourselves, by what entered the heart of mankind after the fall of man. Only true repentance can cleanse our heart and renew a right spirit within us. The pure in heart will see God in all His creation. God wants us to look in the mirror and see ourselves as His beautiful, amazing handiwork.

What lessons can we learn from this? How can we be empowered to overcome the lies of our enemy? First, we must live and remain in the truth of what God has spoken. His truth is the only guarantee of fulfilled promises. We cannot afford to accept lies or any perversion of God's truth because we will suffer the consequences and remain outside the gates of promise.

Second, we must be fully persuaded and committed to trusting the truth that God speaks. If not, we will be easily swayed or tossed to and fro by everyone else's form of truth. We will become double-minded and create a place for evil to come in. The only way we overcome lies or deception is to not make room for them. If we tolerate deception, we make room for it. This includes compromise and conformity as well. To be victorious, we must boldly speak the truth over every lie, or we will be taken captive and lose our inheritance as children of The Most High.

Lastly, we must fervently deal with the effects of sin and recover the vision and purpose God intended us to have. We can no longer remain complacent or apathetic concerning our divine destiny. Our vision was greatly impaired by the effects of sin, and God longs to restore this.

One day the Lord spoke to me and said, *In the Garden of Eden, I gave it all to you. There was no good thing withheld from you. When I said, 'Do not eat of the tree of the knowledge of good and evil,' it was not intended to keep any knowledge or possession from you (referring to mankind).*

There is truly no good thing I will withhold from you. More than anything, I long to bless you. I didn't want you to partake of the fruit of evil because you were not only going to see evil in the world, but you'd also begin to see it in yourself. You'd see flaws and faults, and you'd begin to manipulate and fabricate to keep them covered. Your shame and debasement would cause you to hide in captivity, while blaming others for your pain, insecurities, and dysfunction. You would begin to compare yourselves and compete with one another instead of completing one another.

I knew that anytime you were separated from Me, the true source of your very existence, you'd carry brokenness, rejection and abandonment, and a plethora of other emotional wounds at the core of your being. After all, who you really are is only found in Me, the One who created you. So now I ask you to understand that My plan was, is, and always will be for you to dwell with Me and feast on My goodness. No good thing will I withhold from you, My beloved.

God is so good! He is our Tree of Life that causes us to taste and see the goodness and faithfulness of God. As a matter of fact, He is so faithful that He sent His only Son to die for our failure and unbelief. It was man's lack of judgment, unbridled desires, and unbelief that caused the greatest failure in mankind's history of existence. But God is still faithful and loving no matter what we cause or bring upon ourselves.

In spite of man's sinful behavior, Jesus brought us great restoration and redemption by hanging on a tree. Remember, the Garden of Eden is where we lost everything, including our identity, calling, and eternal inheritance. Adam and Eve sinned against God by eating from that which He had forbidden. Seriously think about that. Mankind broke covenant by eating from the forbidden tree, and Jesus created a way to recover all by dying on a tree. He went right to the place where we failed, so that we could recover all. That's love!

Our challenge now is to see the way that Jesus has prepared for each of us to overcome, obtain victory, and live the abundant life He purchased for us. As sons and daughters of God, we're divinely created to have fellowship with our Father and express His goodness all throughout the earth. We are called to rule with His authority, change lives, and cause the earth to align with the purposes of God. We may have unique functions and spheres of authority, but our heavenly calling will never be taken.

WHAT IS HOLDING YOU BACK?

So now I have a question: What is holding you back? Is it your current home situation? Maybe it's your current employment or the lack thereof? Perhaps the even better question would be: Who, not what, is holding you back?

Could you ever believe a truth that revealed that you are the primary obstacle to your lack of personal advancement or success? It is very possible and likely that you could be the only thing hindering your progress. What if your perception needs to change and not just your less-than-desirable lot in life? What if the resources needed to change your situation have been sitting right in front of you all along?

For example, you might say, "If I only had a car, I would be able to do the thing that I'm most passionate about." Yet you never recognized that you could drive your dad's old car, which is perfectly functional, has a tank full of gasoline, and sits in your parents' garage collecting dust. Honestly speaking, would that be a matter of circumstance or consciousness?

God wants us to awaken and become fully aware of His presence, provision, and victorious, unforeseen strategies as we journey into our divine purposes and destinies. God always has a meticulous, strategic action plan for us to advance and walk into our places of purpose. The Bible says that He always leads us into triumph (see 2 Cor. 2:14), so there's always a prepared way for us to move into divine victory!

Think about that. If ever we feel stuck or defeated in any area of our lives, it is simply because we have not come into an awareness and understanding of God's plan for that specific area. The strategy that God discloses to us becomes our path to victory. In Matthew 6:8 it says the Father knows what we have need of before we ever ask Him.

Therefore do not be like them. For your Father knows the things you have need of before you ask Him.

— Matthew 6:8

This makes Him all the more eager to answer our prayers because He anticipates us coming to Him for our provision. When we know that our Father in Heaven is anticipating and waiting for us to come to Him for provision, we can ask confidently, boldly, and even continually. He promises to supply all our needs.

And my God shall supply all your need according to His riches in glory by Christ Jesus.

— Philippians 4:19

God will also fill us with vision for the provision when we ask. We must understand that asking is connected to our personal level of humility and maturity. It's posturing ourselves to receive the clarity and wisdom we need to establish a certain task or deed. If we are willing to ask, He is always ready to enlighten any darkness within us or deal with any evil that we may face.

For You will light my lamp;
The LORD my God will enlighten my darkness.

— Psalm 18:28

THERE MUST BE REVELATION

Once we recognize what or who is holding us back, we need revelation from the Lord to move forward and prosper. This is why prophetic revelation becomes so very important for each of us. John 6 says:

The Spirit gives life; the flesh counts for nothing.
The words I have spoken to you—they are full of the
Spirit and life.

— John 6:63 NIV

This means the words that are uttered from God's mouth cause new dimensions of life to appear. The unseen becomes visible, and the supernatural manifests in the natural realm.

Prophecy does this. It releases the creative power of the Lord and His kingdom order right into our atmosphere. Then His truth is activated and begins to move in every area of our lives. Prophetic revelation can shift and transform us personally, corporately, or globally, and in some cases, it can be all three. This is how we move from glory to glory.

A revealing of Jesus, the Messiah. God gave it to

*make plain to his servants what is about to happen.
He published and delivered it by Angel to his servant
John. And John told everything he saw: God's
Word— the witness of Jesus Christ!*

— Revelation 1:1-2 MSG

The book of Revelation, written by John the apostle, reveals awesome visions and astonishing details of his interactions as he is taken from the island of Patmos into heavenly realms with the Lord Jesus Christ. By these writings, we witness Jesus' stunning, majestic nature, sovereign power, faithful devotion, and relentless passion toward His people. We can also see the magnificence in the unconventional role He plays in fulfilling the law of love, which is the divine and perfect will of God. Consequently, just as John experienced in that day, God is presently calling out again for His people to come and see the Living Word revealed.

Through the eyes of our understanding, we must continually receive spiritual enlightenment to move into everything God has predestined for us to fulfill. This only happens when we embrace Jesus Christ, the Living Word Himself. When we hear the voice of God speaking to us in our spirit or when reading our Bibles, we receive pure words of truth and power that illuminate the areas of our souls that are darkened and dim. Light breaks forth within us and causes a whole new reality to be formed. Isn't that amazing?

SEEING PAST FAMILIAR KNOWLEDGE

John was a passionate follower of Jesus who later became an apostle to the church in Asia. He is known as "the disciple whom Jesus loved" through his own writings, which are found in the New Testament in the gospel of John. Jesus had to extend a great amount of love, favor, and affirmation toward John for him to feel he was that special! He not only deemed himself to be the Beloved Disciple, but he also wrote a detailed account about it, which has probably been read by people all over the world. Now, that's confidence.

Was he exaggerating? No, I don't think he was exaggerating at all. I believe John moved the heart of Jesus with adoration, worship, and devotion like no one else in the troupe. I presume this is why Jesus chose John as the perfect candidate to communicate the vastness of who He is through the book of Revelation.

Although John already knew Jesus to be the Son of God, the Lord still had to lead John into a greater dimension of wisdom and understanding to reveal the eternal purpose and destiny of His kingdom. He had to come into a greater vision of Jesus—acknowledging who He was and, even more, recognizing who He is and who He is to come.

John, to the seven churches which are in Asia:
Grace to you and peace from Him who is and who
was and who is to come, and from the seven Spirits
who are before His throne.

— Revelation 1:4

God is leading His sons and daughters in this direction. He is taking us away from familiar paradigms of customary, religious practices into extraordinary God-encounters that He has yearned to see manifest from the beginning of time. He has not consented to any lesser form of Christianity.

He wants to see His people moving in the overflow of grace, glory, and power. We are not on the earth to simply exist. We have been perfectly fitted into these specific times to prove and enforce the perfect will of God. May we all awaken and become fully aware of who God is and see how exceptionally well He treats those who love and trust Him.

SURRENDER ALL

When we receive revelation, many times we learn that we must surrender everything to Him to walk with and abide in Him. At one point in my life, I found myself trapped by the familiar. The Lord came to me and ever so gently said, *Robyn, I'm not in your box.*

I gasped and said, "What? What did You say?"

Without hesitation, again He said, *I'm not inside your box. You have a box, and you keep trying to fit Me into it. But I can't fit, and I won't fit. Stop trying to put Me there. It will be better for you to step out of that box than for Me to conform to it.*

Instantly, I began to weep because I love God too much to cause Him to shrink the vastness of who He is into my minute level of understanding. God forbid that I would ever expect Him to conform to my will! I began to yell at the top of my lungs, "God, help me to tear down the walls in my mind and soul that continually attempt to box You in. I don't want my thoughts, emotions, or desires giving me a small, false reality of who You are. I want to know who You really are. Show me, God! Show me!"

As a result of that encounter years ago, I intentionally surrendered everything to embrace something so much greater and to step out on the waters of this incredible journey that I'm allowing the Lord to lead me on. It seems as if I am continually discovering the magnificent splendor of who God really is. His thoughts are beyond astonishing, and His ways are never less than perfect. God will never stop offering us the opportunity to step out and move toward a greater revelation of His covenant plan.

Look at Jeremiah 33:3. The New Living Translation says He

longs to tell remarkable secrets to those who ask of Him. Are you willing to leave the familiar place to see the Lord in a whole new dimension like John the Beloved did? You too are His beloved disciple, and He will reveal the mysteries and riches of His kingdom as you decide to embark on a special journey of seeking the God of love in brand new ways. Are you ready to see what you need to see?

Ask me and I will tell you remarkable secrets you do not know about things to come.

— *Jeremiah 33:3 NLT*

HUMILITY OVERCOMES

Why are revelation and surrendering all to God so important? These create an attitude of humility within us. Our posture of humility serves us to overcome what we encounter in life that prevents us from advancing forward.

What do we do when we are ready to see differently but it seems like nothing we do is working? What happens when chaos and confusion continue to fill the atmosphere and there's no glimpse of light at the end of the tunnel? The problem is we are trying to see through our own eyes through the dark.

It's very hard to see in the dark. God allows us to walk through dark, uncertain times. He lets us feel the discontent and uneasiness of losing the people, things, and systems that give us a false sense of contentment. Yes, He allows this. This is why unexpected situations and events constantly arise in our lives and throw us into various forms of testing and tribulation. As these things unfold, it shakes our sense of normalcy and comfort. When this happens, we humans tend to get fearful and lose confidence. Anxiety rises as our thoughts run all over the place with no sense of faith, hope, or peace.

We will never understand why troubles arise or why other uninvited interruptions occur. But we can gain a greater understanding of who God is and what He has established for us so that we continuously remain buoyant, despite it all.

Asking the Lord for help is humbling. It requires us to acknowledge our need for Him to divinely intervene. This is very important!

> *Ask, and it will be given to you; seek, and you will find; knock, and it will be opened to you. For everyone who asks receives, and he who seeks finds, and to him who knocks it will be opened.*

> — *Matthew 7:7-8*

These things are all predicated on one thing: humility. One of the major keys to overcoming in these uncertain times is humility, especially in today's society. Humility keeps us in a place of continual power and authority for the challenges we are created to confront and overcome. It is the access we need to everything God has for us.

Humility guides us into greatness and steadies us by meekness. It will balance and sustain us. It will lift and promote us. Humility is the golden key to establishing a life of victory.

The Merriam-Webster dictionary gives us the definition of humility as: "freedom from pride or arrogance; the quality or state of being humble." Some synonyms for the word humility include demureness, down-to-earthness, lowliness, meekness, and modesty. When we rid ourselves of pride or arrogance, we consequently take on the state of being humble. Humility will be at the foundation of our character when we are free from pride and haughtiness.

Best-selling author and pastor Rick Warren wrote, "Humility is not thinking less of yourself, it's thinking of yourself less." In other words, humility is not self-debasement, it's servanthood. When we are humble, we take the role or position of a servant, and we look to meet the needs of someone else. Having the heart of a servant postures us to receive His power, not our own. It gives us entry into dimensions and places where we don't normally have access.

> *For* as *the heavens are higher than the earth,*
> *So are My ways higher than your ways,*
> *And My thoughts than your thoughts.*

> — *Isaiah 55:9*

When we are humble, we can resist pride and stubbornness. We can say, "I'm willing to lower myself to gain a higher perspective and become the necessary instrument or vessel for the assignment without bias, preference, or ego. I have no other posture but to become what is necessary for the will of God to be demonstrated."

I can remember one day when my husband and I were having a strong disagreement. God spoke to me about this concept of humility. In a very heated moment, He stepped in and said, *Robyn, do you want to win the argument, or do you want to win the war? The war is against your marriage, your children, your future posterity, and the generational blessing in your bloodline.*

That put it all into perspective for me. I achieved a higher viewpoint because I saw past my ego, and I knew at that moment that I had to decide. Would I choose to be right or righteous? Righteousness is acting in accordance with what God requires or desires. I chose to humble myself and move into the righteousness that God desired.

We must choose this standpoint of humility every single day to truly walk in victory. If we have a pure heart along with pure motives, we will walk in the integrity, servanthood, and submission it takes to overcome the trials of life. Submission and humility work together like teammates. When we are humble, we join the winning team, and we make the winning plays because of our submission.

A person who is willing to embrace submission understands that there is a greater task at hand with a greater outcome for a greater purpose than their own. They subdue their opposing attitudes as they come into alignment and agreement for a greater good. A submitted person lays down their limited mindset or viewpoint to serve the higher way and the larger objective for greater impact and effective results.

Jesus is King and He has a kingdom. That kingdom has its own governance and its own spiritual laws. Those laws establish His kingdom in the earth. Therefore, when we are completely submitted to His plan, we will seek the ways of His kingdom. This gives us full access to His power and authority so that we may confidently declare, "Your kingdom come, and Your will be done on earth as it is in heaven!"

In this hour, The Lord is resetting and realigning us with His divine purpose. He is still advancing His plan, no matter what is happening in the earth right now. He is the Master Builder who is still building and assembling His church. Sons and daughters of God must understand the significance of humility and submission.

When we come under submission to the Maker of heaven and earth, that posture of humility causes us to gain the vision and heart of the Almighty. This repositions us and allows us to enter the divine mandate that we were created to walk in and fulfill.

The more we are filled with the heart of God, the more we

will understand His objectives for our lives. When we humble ourselves to receive from Him, we can see the vastness of His power and dominion. This gives us the faith and confidence we need to do what we're predestined to do on behalf of our families, workplaces, and communities.

Here's the danger: We have a choice. We can choose to forge our own path or trust the One who put us on the path. This is addressed in Proverbs:

> *Do not be wise in your own eyes;*
> *Fear the LORD and depart from evil.*

> *— Proverbs 3:7*

When we look at this Scripture, we can see King Saul did not embrace this truth. He decided to do what He desired instead of doing what the Lord had commanded of him. He stopped submitting to the instructions of the Lord and forged his own path by leaning to his own understanding. One moment of pride and rebellion repositioned Saul's destiny and placed him on the path of destruction.

In the thirteenth chapter of the book of Samuel, Samuel said to Saul,

> *You have done foolishly. You have not kept the commandment of the LORD your God, which He commanded you. For now the LORD would have established your kingdom over Israel forever. But now your kingdom shall not continue. The LORD has sought for Himself a man after His own heart, and the LORD has commanded him to be commander over His people, because you have not kept what the*

LORD commanded you.

— 1 Samuel 13:13-14

Our human wisdom will never measure up. The way we desire to do things will never fulfill the desire of God. His ways will always yield the greater outcome because He alone is God.

Saul learned a big lesson that day. He learned that leaning on his own understanding caused him to go down a very different path than the one God desired for him. Learning to love God and to know Him will create desire for His wisdom and His ways. This is why He says to love Him with all of our heart, all of our soul, all of our mind, and all of our strength (see Mark 12:30).

In this, we can make a divine exchange. When we give Him all of our heart, soul, mind, and strength we receive all of God's heart, vision, wisdom, and strength. God's vision is masterful, and it empowers us to master difficult things. This is how we overcome!

To see our way out, we must see through God's eyes and His ways. This requires His revelation, which may mean looking at situations and circumstances differently. When we humble ourselves and submit to His ways, we will always see the way out because we are seeing from His omniscient perspective. Humility enables us to receive His revealed truth and stand on it, no matter what we may face. Come hell or high water, we are not moved!

MEDITATION FOR APPLICATION

Set aside 15-30 minutes each day to commune with God. Each day read and meditate on one of the Scriptures listed below. Follow these steps.

1. Get in a quiet place without distraction.

2. Play a praise song and just listen to the words.

3. Ask God to reveal His heart and meaning to you as you read the Scriptures.

4. Write your reflections below or in your journal.

5. Read the Scriptures daily so you receive maximum revelation.

Psalm 1:1-3 TPT
Genesis 3:7 NKJV
Philippians 4:19 NKJV
Isaiah 55:9 NKJV

MOMENTS OF REFLECTION

1. What is familiar to you in the way that you relate to God or see your role in His kingdom? How does that hold you back from seeing past old ways of thinking?

2. What lie has the enemy told you that causes you to doubt that God is a good father with your best in mind?

3. Seek the Lord to help you see His ways that are higher and better than your ways. What can you change in your perspective of the world and the people in your life? How will this impact you in a positive way?

4. How can you mature in faith to truly believe that God will always provide everything you need?

Notes:

CHAPTER 3
RECIEVE THE TRUTH AND STAND

The core of our entire being is established on the truth of God's love for us, but we must agree with it to see it manifest. Who we are is not what we do. There are times that we may believe the lies of others and begin to question who we are, but that does not change the person God predestined and created. Let's look at the story of creation to see the deep truth of God's love for us.

> *In the beginning God created the heavens and the earth.*
>
> *— Genesis 1:1 NLT*

In the beginning, there was God—the all-seeing and -knowing God, the all-powerful God, the omnipresent God, the One who was hovering and drawing near to the darkness and chaos of existence. Love Himself was bringing a new order to that which knew no love.

Over and over, He created something beautiful out of nothing. When He spoke His heart's desire, His breath was released upon it, and suddenly it appeared. It was there, just like He said. He looked upon all its beauty and said, "It is good."

And on the sixth day, when God created man, He drew close to the Earth which He had made and formed man from the dust. He breathed His breath into his nostrils and man came alive! He then took a portion from Adam and created a woman called Eve. On that day He looked upon His creation with great joy and enthusiasm and declared to the heavens and the earth, "This is very good!"

> *For by Him all things were created that are in heaven and that are on earth, visible and invisible, whether thrones or dominions or principalities or powers. All things were created through Him and for Him. And He is before all things, and in Him all things consist.*
>
> — *Colossians 1:16-17*

Adam and Eve were chosen by God as a prototype for all of humanity. They were the ones whom God loved, the ones that all of the earth would see as blessed and highly favored by God.

The serpent deterred this for a moment by challenging what God had created in the Garden. But now, through the blood of Christ, we are given the opportunity to stand in the place of God's loving truth and receive that truth for every broken or fallen place in our lives. The absolute truth of God's love for us is already established without consent or agreement, but we still must choose to agree with it or not. It is unyielding, unwavering, and completely immutable, from generation to generation.

When truth is established in our heart, we receive it through the knowledge of God's love. Our soul is in full agreement with a greater force or dynamic that is unshakable; we are fully convinced or convicted by what has been communicated through word or action. Ideologies, facts, and situations cannot cause a person who holds fast to the truth to swerve because they recognize that there is a higher dynamic in operation.

HIS WORD IS THE SOLID TRUTH

He will delight in obeying the LORD.
He will not judge by appearance
nor make a decision based on hearsay.

— Isaiah 11:3 NLT

In the Bible, Caleb and Joshua did not walk by what they saw or heard. Unlike the other spies who were sent to spy out the land of Canaan, they walked by the truth of their covenant-keeping God. He had spoken and promised to give them the land, and they believed it. Everything that the Lord spoke to them was established. Their agreement with God's loving truth and strict obedience caused them to overcome the giants in the land. Agreeing with God produced the faith they needed to overcome every difficulty they would ever face. Many times we don't recognize that we ignorantly adhere to cultural and traditional beliefs that chop away at the truth of our identity and prophetic destiny. In truth, we are powerful, creative beings working with the Eternal One to establish His eternal purposes.

Recently, I was watching a game show where participants were given a question with three multiple choice answers to choose from. The host posed a question and asked for the correct answer. The question was: "For health and safety, how long should you wait after you have eaten to get back into a swimming pool?" The answers were: a) forty-five minutes, b) thirty minutes, and c) you don't have to wait.

All three of the contestants openly verbalized their thought process and spoke how they were leaning toward "b" because their parents had taught them to wait at least thirty minutes before getting into a swimming pool after eating food. I also remembered that many people in my life had told me

39

the same thing. Somehow, though, I knew the answer was "c": You don't have to wait. While waiting to hear the correct answer, I told my husband, "I think we've all been given a myth to live by throughout the generations, and we all adhere to it as if it's the truth."

The game show host finally read the answer. As suspected, the answer was "c." Almost everyone in my house got it wrong. I was the one person who thought that what had been traditionally spoken to all of us could possibly not be correct. Everyone else stood firm on what they had been taught.

People often do what they have been told simply because they were taught to honor and respect the person who told it to them. However, it isn't necessarily true just because it came from an honorable source. God's truth and our truth are two very different concepts. God's truth is not only factual but also eternal.

Our truth is based on feelings, logic, and facts. God's truth is based on the knowledge of who He is, which includes His power, wisdom, and covenant with men. Our truth is a very diluted or distorted form of His truth. When we water down the words of Holy God, we don't simply dilute them, we also pollute them and produce a different truth. Every time we add our opinion, idea, or perspective to the Word of God, we dilute the greatness of the pure and holy, and we get a different outcome than what God intended. This dilution creates a mixture, distortion, and compromise in our homes, relationships, and society as a whole.

> *But God's truth stands firm like a foundation stone with this inscription: "The LORD knows those who are his," and "All who belong to the LORD must turn away from evil."*
>
> *— 2 Timothy 2:19 NLT*

Therefore whoever hears these sayings of Mine, and
does them, I will liken him to a wise man who built
his house on the rock: and the rain descended, the
floods came, and the winds blew and beat on that
house; and it did not fall, for it was founded on the
rock. But everyone who hears these sayings of Mine,
and does not do them, will be like a foolish man who
built his house on the sand.

— *Matthew 7:24-26*

When we receive or accept a lesser version of the truth because it keeps us comfortable or secure, we miss God's power and purpose. We like to hear things that make us feel good about ourselves and don't necessarily ruffle our feathers. We don't care to hear those truthful words that upset us, ruin our day, or bruise our egos. But those words are just as important as the encouraging words. They allow us to do a quick course correction whenever we veer off the path of destiny and promise.

God's truth continually infuses us with overcoming power for whatever we may face. Once again, it may not always feel good to our flesh, but it continually liberates us to move into a better place. His words rescue us from some of the worst mistakes and decisions we'll ever make, while stabilizing and establishing a new footing for us to thrive. Then we can evolve, mature, and see what we need to live a happy, blessed, and fulfilled life.

THE GOOD, THE BAD, AND THE UGLY TRUTH

A few years ago, I was in the car running errands, getting ready to go on a ministry trip to Tennessee. It was a normal day full of normal activities, but God decided it was a good time to abruptly interrupt my sense of normalcy

While I was driving, I heard the Lord say, *Robyn, it is never My will for you to walk blindly. I do not want you to be ignorant. You must begin to desire the fullness of truth and allow yourself to bear it. My desire is to show you the good, the bad, and the ugly, so My Church will be victorious. You must watch and pray as I reveal the truth.*

I felt the Lord was saying the same thing to me that Jack Nicholson's character, Colonel Jessup, shouted at Tom Cruise in the 1992 film *A Few Good Men* when he exclaimed, "You can't handle the truth!" What the Lord said greatly disturbed me because I have lived most of my Christian life with a strong desire to be one with the Lord in all things. Suddenly, it seemed like there was a separation, almost like we were in two totally different places. I had come face to face with the truth, the truth that I had a form of godliness, a false representation that completely limited God from doing more than I could ask or think.

I knew I had to change. I knew I had to become more pliable in my perception and belief system. After all, the only obstructions pointed directly to me. My own thoughts, ideas, and belief systems had been fashioned by worldly structures that I had to overcome. I desperately wanted Him to know that He could freely share His heart with me. I wanted to know His deepest secrets and desires. So I chose to see. I exercised my will and chose to see everything, even those things I did not want to see.

I began to allow God to stretch me and break down all sorts of false ideologies and vain imaginations. I allowed Him to show me the good, the bad, and the ugly as He so desired. He revealed the angels and the demons, the fragrant and the putrid, the truth and the lies. He woke me up with unimaginable dreams that led me to pray for hours. It was not "the sweet by and by." As a matter of fact, the sweet by and by had quickly gone bye-bye.

God revealed more and more truth to me on a daily basis. I never questioned why; I simply prayed. I knew He was revealing it to me so I could call on Him to get involved. My key role was to invoke the power and presence of God no matter how good, how bad, or how ugly the situation seemed. His role was to bring redemption, justice, and restoration. I'm so thankful that I stopped walking blindly long enough to see God glorified in greater ways. I learned that I can handle the truth when I allow it to work in me.

Truth has a weight to it. We often have the propensity to water down or lighten up the truth of a matter because we don't like feeling the weight of a heavy situation. Let's face it, five- or ten-pound weights are much easier to carry than fifty- to one-hundred-pound weights. I can do more repetitions, keep my energy up, exercise longer, and feel like Superwoman if I'm only using ten-pound weights. However, if I try to do the same routines with one-hundred-pound weights, I can almost guarantee that it will not be enjoyable for me.

This is how most of us deal with the truth in life. We tend to deal with weighty matters just enough to lift the burden, or weight, never getting to the root or truth of the matter. Still, God is faithful to allow the truth to continue to surface so He can heal every area of our lives, which takes us into divine freedom. His unyielding pursuit is always justified by a pure desire to see His children triumph over their enemy.

THE WAY, THE TRUTH, AND THE LIFE

Let's look at one of Jesus' most faithful followers, formerly known as Simon. Simon started out as a fisherman but quickly rose to become one of the most influential leaders in the New

Testament Church. He was one of Jesus' most devoted disciples and closest friends. He walked in tremendous authority and power and performed great miracles, but he also had to be set free from his carnal mind and old identity. Walking with the Messiah caused him to face the truth of who he was, who he wasn't, and who he was meant to become.

In Matthew 16, Simon received a divine revelation from his heavenly Father that Jesus was truly the Messiah, the Son of the Living God. He was spiritual enough to recognize the Christ and understand the will of God. Jesus affirmed Simon, in the company of all the other disciples, for speaking such truth. He then told Simon his true identity and prophetic destiny, while giving him a limitless measure of power and authority to demonstrate the kingdom of heaven at will. From that moment forward, he was known as Peter.

Peter was devoted, but very presumptuous. He was zealous, but impulsive. And although he was spiritual, he was also very carnal. He would find himself humbled and humiliated because of his natural tendencies. The only way he could overcome those fleshly impulses and reactions was by Jesus revealing the truth.

And you will know the truth, and the truth will set you free.

— John 8:32 NLT

Matthew 16:23 provides a different picture of Peter. Not long after Jesus publicly commended Peter for receiving the divine revelation of the Messiah, He turned and rebuked Satan for speaking through Peter. Jesus took this same moment to speak some truth to His disciples, so they'd gain understanding about their calling.

But He turned and said to Peter, "Get behind Me, Satan! You are an offense to Me, for you are not mindful of the things of God, but the things of men."

— *Matthew 16:23*

Essentially what the Lord was saying is, "If any of you wants to be My follower, you must give up your own way, take up your cross, and follow Me." He was letting them know that their way would give access to Satan. This would cause them to veer away from the path of God and produce a major stumbling block to the divine purposes of Father God.

Over and over, Jesus had to declare the truth to Peter so that he could be enlightened and freed from his personal bondages and wrong mindsets. Jesus revealed to Peter that he would betray Him three times. Peter wrongly assumed that he would be willing to faithfully follow anywhere. He didn't realize that his heart was filled with pride and presumption, until he betrayed Jesus three times, just as the Lord had spoken.

Throughout the journey as a disciple, Peter was continually being liberated from erroneous beliefs and attitudes. Although he may not have always seen things accurately, he allowed the truth to settle in his heart and make him free. He humbly embraced the words of his teacher and quickly repented of his misguided ways and fleshly propensities. These trials and testings produced a new identity in Peter. He received a tremendous amount of revelation that has led others into a deeper knowledge of Christ for generations. He learned to walk in humility and wisdom that would be instrumental for the equipping of the Church.

I don't think it was a coincidence that Peter received the opportunity to walk on water when he showed a desire to step out of the boat. He had the faith and courage, but he needed the truth to stand on when the winds and waves started. Peter's name means Rock. God wanted Peter to become steadfast and immovable. And even now I believe that the Lord desires to have a people who will be so fastened to Him that the winds and waves swirling in the world today will not deter them. Their lives will be built on God's truth alone, and the gates of hell shall not prevail!

Wherever we are headed in this new era will take great faith, but we must stand on the truth of God's Word and live by it to be completely unshakeable. Like Peter, God will reveal who we truly are. This new identity will only be established by the truth of God. It is greater than anything we have ever imagined about ourselves. It is personal, it is intimate, and it is true.

Jesus is the way, the truth, and the life. We must walk in His ways, receive His truth, and follow Him into new life. His truth is where we abide. His truth is where we stand. His truth is where we remain.

At a particular time, the Lord allowed me to walk through one of the most challenging circumstances I have ever faced. I ask that you hear this testimony with an open heart, a heart without judgment, criticism, or analysis. Put your measuring stick away and allow God to reveal what it is you need to receive in your heart from this testimony.

AN OCTOBER DAY THAT CHANGED MY PERSPECTIVE

I'll start by sharing that I hear the voice of God when He speaks to me. I know who He is and how He speaks to me. I've heard His voice from the moment I came into relationship with Him in the mid-1990's. When I hear Him, I am compelled to listen and obey. His words hold great weight in my life because He has proven to me repeatedly that His promises are true.

On this normal day in October of 2014, I was driving my

car with my two youngest kids in the backseat. Just as we had done every single day, we were on our way to pick up their oldest brother, who was in high school at the time. On this day I heard the Lord say, *Pull over and fasten your seat belts and make sure the kids are strapped in.* So I pulled over in front of a bank and did exactly that. Right after that, my kids pleaded with me to buy them frozen Slurpee drinks. I said "Sure!" So we got the drinks and were quickly back on the road.

Now I was running a tad behind. What I didn't realize in that moment was that I had rushed back into the vehicle without strapping myself in. Two minutes later, I was hit by another vehicle and ejected from mine. I was told by witnesses that the car flipped three times and was utterly destroyed. Yet my kids remained calm and walked away without a single scratch!

I woke up in the hospital the next day wondering about the huge cast that extended from over my knee to the bottom of my foot along with the severe road rash all over my back. Strangely enough, I did not remember much about the accident because it all seemed to be a blur. I knew I had had a car accident, but I did not remember much else. I had had emergency surgery to repair my ankle that had been broken in ten places, which explained the huge cast.

After I was released from the hospital, I was placed on bed rest for six weeks to stay off the ankle while it was healing. Then I had to bravely prepare myself to walk again. I knew the road ahead was not going to be easy, by any means. I had to be courageous and face whatever I needed to do so I'd have the ability to walk again. I was determined to press through that excruciating pain to get myself into a place of wholeness.

While struggling with the emotional and mental instability of this situation, I had to be willing and teachable if I wanted to be whole again. Keep in mind, I had been bedridden for almost two months. So before I could even think about walking, I had to learn to stand. Although it hurt me tremendously, I had to press through the pain so I could begin to put pressure on my ankle and stand on my own. Then I started my physical therapy sessions.

When I began physical therapy, I realized that this was not going to be easy or pleasant in any way. I had to learn new things, depend on people more, and deal with the pain instead of escaping it. This stretched me beyond all limits. Honestly, I felt that physical therapy made me look like a fool because of the extremely painful and exaggerated movements I had to make. So I decided to walk the way I felt comfortable walking.

One day the physical therapist said, "Let me be honest with you. You're hurting yourself by doing it like that. The way you're trying to walk will not help you heal properly or progress, because you're throwing your weight in one direction. You're training yourself to walk improperly." God added, *Robyn, you have to humble yourself and receive instruction to walk in My calling for your life. You have never been this way before, and you don't know how to walk just yet.* This shifted my mindset, and I began to do what I needed to do to walk in wisdom for a brighter future.

A NEW WAY OF VICTORY

When the physical therapist gave me those strong words of correction, I received it. I knew he was giving me something to stand on. He wasn't telling me what I wanted to hear, and he surely wasn't agreeing with my way of seeing it. It was the truth I needed to hear at that time, so I could not only stand but also step in the right way into my future. When I changed my perspective, I was able to do the necessary internal work to physically walk into victory and overcome my mental and emotional obstacles. It completely transformed me.

We must receive God's truth to walk in faith and establish new victories in our lives. We may not be able to see in the natural realm the results of doing what He instructs us to do, even if it is painful. However, we must have faith to know He is guiding us to do what will benefit us the most in the long term.

God wants the same for each of us. To become unstoppable and unshakeable, we must embrace the truth of God and those He sends to help us become whole. We can't live by our feelings and think that we are doing God's will. That is deception. Our feelings will trick us and begin to dictate our every move. We cannot allow that.

When we are moving according to our feelings and making decisions according to them, we are not following the leading of the Holy Spirit. God's Spirit, which is the Spirit of Truth, causes us to overcome our feelings and see the way forward. That's the goal.

> *Jesus answered, "I am the way and the truth and the life. No one comes to the Father except through me."*
>
> *— John 14:6 NIV*

That's what we want. We want to move forward successfully and victoriously, remaining in the center of God's will. When we find Jesus, we find that strong, immovable rock we need to boldly stand and take our place in the earth realm. God's unshakeable kingdom begins to manifest in us, through us, and all around us.

> *Because of this, you must wear all the armor that God provides so you're protected as you confront the slanderer, for you are destined for all things and will rise victorious. Put on truth as a belt to strengthen you to stand in triumph.*
>
> *— Ephesians 6:13-14 TPT*

Look at those words. "You must wear all the armor that God provides!" Selah.

MEDITATION FOR APPLICATION

Set aside 15-30 minutes each day to commune with God. Each day read and meditate on one of the Scriptures listed below. Follow these steps.

1. Get in a quiet place without distraction.

2. Play a praise song and just listen to the words.

3. Ask God to reveal His heart and meaning to you as you read the Scriptures.

4. Write your reflections below or in your journal.

5. Read the Scriptures daily so you receive maximum revelation.

Colossians 1:16-17 NKJV
2 Timothy 2:19 NLT
Ephesians 6:13-14 TPT

MOMENTS OF REFLECTION

1. Is there an area of life where it's hard for you to face the truth? Why? Remember, nothing is too hard for God to handle.

2. Write down the good, the bad, and the ugly about that truth. Then give this to the Lord and ask Him for the strength to deal with it.

Notes:

Chapter 4
Expose the Deception of Fear

How we stand in this life ultimately determines the course for the future. Even though we know that standing on the truth and living by God's truth enrich our lives, the deception of fear can block that. Our principles, beliefs, actions, and, yes, even our fears, are key factors for how we choose to stand in our lifetime.

Fear works against us and weakens our stand. Fear causes us to question the truth we believe and compels us to move in a different direction, away from the plan of God. We must expose the trickery of fear because fear deceives the mind and causes a different belief to rise up. Sometimes we agree with our fears, which breeds deception, and deception alters our beliefs. This becomes very dangerous because *we are what we believe.*

For as he thinketh within himself, so is he.

— Proverbs 23:7 ASV

We are going to gain understanding about these distorted belief systems that hold us back or give us a wrong view of who we truly are. Many of us suffer with wrong beliefs about ourselves right now. We need to identify what is crippling us or keeping us from succeeding and advancing.

What voice is speaking to you and telling you that you can't or won't do something? What causes you to see something that only appears when your comfort and safety levels are challenged? Are you so blindly devoted to your belief system that you can't realize it's the very thing that is crippling you?

Worry, distrust, and anxiety can stir our emotions, thus presenting a false narrative and a distorted reality of God's will for our lives. Sometimes I hear people say, "I think God wants me to have this, so I'm going to go after it," or "I believe that God wants me to do this, so I'm going to just do it." They make false assumptions about what God wants for them because they are subconsciously pacifying the fears that are rooted in their hearts.

For example, if God promised that you would one day own a vineyard that you did not plant and a house you did not build, does it mean you should move to Napa Valley, California, because the region is known for its beautiful houses and gorgeous vineyards? What if He sends you to Texas instead? Are you going to be okay with that? Wrong expectations and beliefs can cause us to create or remain in cycles of dysfunction. Fearing that we won't get what we want, we create the narrative that is most conducive to our own desires.

Prophetic words can also be perverted by the underlying fears in a person's soul, causing a twisted interpretation. As a result, what is said by the speaker and what is heard by the listener can be two very different statements. It's possible to get completely off track by holding too tightly to the promises of God. Steadfast faith can easily turn into worry and fear when we allow the prophecy to become the driving force in our life. We must follow the Promise Keeper rather than the promise.

Now hope does not disappoint, because the love of God has been poured out in our hearts by the Holy Spirit who was given to us.

— Romans 5:5

Deferred hope comes on us when we begin to pursue promises instead of the Promise Keeper. Our wrong, fearful expectations may lead us into hopelessness and disappointment, but hope in God does not. Personally, I don't suffer with the issue of hope deferred because I continue to follow the One who is my Living Hope. He is the living, eternal hope who never disappoints us.

God's presence is our plan and it's a sure plan. When we listen to the voice that says we must build a nest egg or we must have a plan B and C, we negate the power of God's love and His provision for us. We must defeat the voice of "what if." We cannot strategize, calculate, or prepare more than God. Fear will cause us to believe that we can do more than God, and this will quickly lead us into error. That is what we call deception. If we believe for a moment that our ability matches or exceeds God's ability to supply our need or create the path of advancement, then we are deceived by our own thoughts. This will cause us to react in fear instead of acting in faith.

God is enough. His strength is made perfect when we are at our weakest point. He will become our way of breakthrough and the answer to every problem. He is the absolute truth and definite solution to every place of fear, trepidation, and uncertainty that comes along. We must tell ourselves this truth and stand upon it: "He is powerful enough to establish every detail of my entire life and deliver me from every trouble."

Here is an example. My mom and my dad were two very different people, so different that it was like one was night and the other was day. Although they were legally separated in my early years, they were very successful at giving me an incredible foundation of love and faith while I was growing up, which I certainly did not realize at that time.

When I was faced with something unfamiliar, uncomfortable, or just downright frightening, my dad would always push me toward my fears instead of rescuing me from them. He would say to me, "Do it. Go ahead, Robyn! You can do it."

Understand, he was saying that from a place of faith and love, and even experience. He would continue by saying, "I'm not going to let you fall or hurt yourself, so do it. Just do it, my girl." Consequently, this left no room for fear at all. When Daddy said, "Just do it," I did! If any sort of fear was present, I would swiftly adjust because Daddy wasn't playing games. He was soft-spoken but firm. I had to quickly conquer my fears with strict obedience; I didn't have any options other than to obey. This is clearly how we should respond to any challenging circumstance, as we listen to the words of our heavenly Father resounding in our hearts.

Here's another example in the gospels of the New Testament. Jesus told the disciples, "Go and heal the sick." They immediately did it because they had full faith in the love of Jesus for them. Once again, fear had no place in them. They knew He would never lie to them or cause them to fail or fall. There was no lie or guile within Him or the words that He spoke. His motives were pure, and His expectations were good. His perfect love displaced every area of fear and empowered them to become mighty men of God.

Here's the truth. Many of us tend to accept dysfunction, disorder, compromise, or a lesser portion of living because of our fear. Our worldly systems have taught us that this way of low living is normal. Our religious, educational, and governmental systems have taught us that if we just comply, we have no need for faith in the truth of God's Word or His faithfulness. We only need to do what we're told.

The problem with this abased way of living is that, if we follow it, we will never experience the greatness of God's plan. We must always remember that God leads us into every blessing and promise by faith. We must have faith to submit or faith to trust or even faith to obey the Lord's instructions. Even when we're afraid, it is our acts of faith that cause us to advance and break away from fearful habits. Fear will limit us and cause us to live habitually with a false sense of peace, comfort, and safety.

This anxious, limited, fear-based lifestyle can affect our goal setting, aspirations, marriage, parenting, mentoring, or ministry. It will keep us boxed in. We will operate out of the same measure of ability we've always had, with the same mindset for the same function or purpose. It gives no room for growth, increase, or enlargement.

Recently, dear friends of mine went to another country on a ministry trip. Before they left, we were praying for our spiritual daughter who was a part of the team going on this trip. I felt compelled by the Holy Spirit to tell her, "Do not limit God. God is not apostolic or prophetic; He is so much more than that! We need those labels, words, or phrases to identify various aspects of what He is doing in our midst according to our miniscule perception, not His." I told her, "Do not limit God. Let Him have His way. We have seen God do so many miracles on ministry trips because we don't limit Him in how He can move. We let Him move however He wants to move. He doesn't have to be prophetic or apostolic. He can do whatever."

When she came back from the trip, she gave us a very good report. She said she had been blown away. She had gotten sick on the trip and hadn't been able to operate within her usual capacity of ministry as a powerful, gifted worship leader. This forced her to make room for God. She had to do something new when she took a backseat to flow with their worship team. Simultaneously, this caused everyone else on the team to abandon the familiar and step into a new place. This also meant God could do whatever He wanted. It wound up creating the atmosphere for miracles. People were healed, delivered, and realigned with God! A new season opened for many because the safety of the familiar was taken away.

We can experience the same types of breakthroughs if we stop limiting God. If we will simply walk by faith and not by sight, feelings, or "what if," then we will see the promises of God begin to unfold on our own path. Fear is a lie that produces instability, insecurity, and hopeless narratives. It really is a lie. If we are going to overcome the things that weaken us, we must acknowledge what it is at the root level. We must identify what is robbing and opposing us so we can arrest and dismantle those things. This is how we recover what belongs to us and become who we're meant to be. Truth and love prevail when fear is exposed, cast down, and cut off.

STAND ON THE TRUTH

Seeing the truth and knowing the truth are two very different things. For instance, we can pass daily by a package that has been sitting on our doorstep for months without ever recognizing it belongs to us. If we don't bend down to get a closer look and recognize that it has our name written on it, then most likely we will not approach it, embrace it, or use it. Ultimately, we will forfeit all the benefits of possessing whatever is inside that package.

A familiar saying that many toss around is "Those who know better, do better." But that is not necessarily always the case. Many times we know better, but we choose to do differently. In other words, we can know the truth but never embrace it or agree with it. For instance, I can theoretically know that physical exercise is good for my body, but that doesn't mean I exercise as I should.

When we see the truth, we gain understanding and recognize a greater reality. When we agree with that truth, we step into action. It is only by agreement and its accompanying action that we will manifest that truth. True agreement enables us to embrace and access everything that is being revealed.

THE LIE

Fear is the only thing that will stop us from standing on God's truth or taking that next step toward God's plan. When we fear, it causes us to feel weak, hopeless, helpless, and incapable, forfeiting our God-given authority and power.

Fear is one of our worst enemies, and Satan uses it as one of his greatest weapons against humanity. It alters, weakens, and defiles every area of our life when we allow it to have access. It changes our identity, relationships, and perception, leaving us living in the shadows of others.

Fear is a harsh dictator because it controls and manipulates every part of our life. It sets the order and rules for how we operate within its confinement. It tells us what we can and cannot do. Fear never takes into consideration our potential, capabilities, talents or giftings, and it certainly doesn't consider the fact that God has already created and chosen us for a specific purpose. Fear causes us to dread the outcome ahead. That's the opposite of what God wants for us.

Fear leads to insecurity, which opens the door to a variety of emotional reactions. Some of those are jealousy, envy, anger, competition, and unhealthy comparison. When we feel insecure, we feel inadequate and unsure of who we are and what we can accomplish. Without cutting off the root of fear, we'll live a life driven by one or more of those negative feelings.

Unresolved negativity turns into bad habits, and bad habits turn into painfully unhealthy cycles. For instance, fear of rejection can cause people to move into rebellion, and rebellion can result in control and manipulation. This destructive rejection-rebellion-control cycle cannot be overcome until rejection is dealt with.

For example, we may look at someone and determine within ourselves that we can't trust that person because they may potentially become a threat or some form of trouble to us. So we quickly conclude that they are not a part of our tribe or circle, and we begin to distance ourselves from them. In instances like this, remember that the point of origin begins with us. We begin to listen to the fears of our own heart, not the wickedness of theirs. Our emotions take over and we come to a false conclusion based on the conversation in our head.

That is not how we express love to those we don't know; distancing ourselves comes from a person who is broken and driven by the root of fear. Remember, there is no fear in love. Love casts fear out! Love invites people (and all their baggage) into a space so that we can truly get to know them. This allows us to have an accurate account instead of prejudging them.

> *There is no fear in love; but perfect love casts out fear, because fear involves torment. But he who fears has not been made perfect in love.*
>
> — *1 John 4:18*

Let's look at some common fears that create inaccurate perceptions and dysfunctional habits. This will help us gain more insight into the internal struggles we face on a regular basis and loose us from the grip of fear.

TYPES OF FEAR

REJECTION

Fear of rejection causes us to move into cycles of self-defense, pride, and rebellion. As a result, we build an emotional wall of defense that is dysfunctional and creates unnecessary confusion and chaos for those around us. We use control, manipulation, and deceit to defend ourselves. These cycles will not be broken until the rejection is acknowledged and addressed with loving truth.

MAN

When we suffer from the fear of man, we fear what other people may think or how they may respond. The opinion of a man or woman is exalted higher than it should be, and it causes a fear of others' responses or reactions. This can lead to lack of identity, wrong relationships, and divided loyalty.

FAILURE

We experience fear of failure when we are faced with a challenge that has the potential to negatively affect the future. Instead of moving forward in a reasonable way, we may pass up opportunities to grow and prosper.

SUCCESS

When we fear success, we carry anxiety or nervousness over the moment we apprehend or achieve something new. We immediately become nervous over the responsibility of making sure that we maintain success. The very thought of having to sustain what is successfully achieved begins to torment our mind.

OUR DEEPEST FEAR

Marianne Williamson wrote a book called *A Return to Love*, and an excerpt has become famous. The passage is not a typical, romanticized piece that places us in beautiful scenery with graceful words, while you hear the imaginary violin playing in the background. On the contrary, the quotation is up close, personal, and revealing. It elicits intimate and uncomfortable feelings. It embodies truth, exposure, vulnerability, strength, exhortation, and enlightenment all at the same time. It is profound.

Our deepest fear is not that we are inadequate. Our deepest fear is that we are powerful beyond measure. It is our light, not our darkness, that most frightens us. We ask ourselves, Who am I to be brilliant, gorgeous, talented, and fabulous? Actually, who are you not to be? You are a child of God. Your playing small doesn't serve the world. There's nothing enlightened about shrinking so that other people won't feel insecure around you. We are all meant to shine, as children do. We were born to manifest the glory of God that is within us. It's not just some of us; it's in everyone. And as we let our own light shine, we unconsciously give other people permission to do the same. As we are liberated from our own fear, our presence automatically liberates others.

DEFEAT FEAR

If we are tormented by voices of fear, insecurity, rejection, intimidation, or any other self-abasing spirit, declare, "I am chosen and accepted by my Father! My Father loves me! He is working out the details of my life for my good. I will see His mighty delivering power wipe away all of my fears!"

Now I decree over you: *Your time to rise up is now! Seek the Lord and ask Him to take you beyond your present dwelling place. Your winter has passed, and the storm is over. Nothing can hold you back. It's a new day! You've made it through!*

The Lord is saying to us, *Determine today if you're going to be tied down and bound by fear, fear of man, rejection, or failure. Will you be bound by insecurities and doubt, afraid to believe? Or will you rise up as a son or daughter of the Kingdom?*

God wants to take us to new places. He's ready to give us revelation and a new vision with fresh perspective and ideas.

The Lord of heaven's armies is strongly exhorting each of us. He's saying, *Do not fear! I am with you now, and I will be with you tomorrow. Let Me show you My ways. I will establish your footing and keep you in perfect peace as you rise and follow Me. Your enemies will be My enemies and I will cause them to come down, but you will progress and prosper as My faithful child.*

MEDITATION FOR APPLICATION

Set aside 15-30 minutes each day to commune with God. Each day read and meditate on one of the Scriptures listed below. Follow these steps.

1. Get in a quiet place without distraction.

2. Play a praise song and just listen to the words.

3. Ask God to reveal His heart and meaning to you as you read the Scriptures.

4. Write your reflections below or in your journal.

5. Read the Scriptures daily so you receive maximum revelation.

1 John 4:18 NKJV
Proverbs 23:7 ASV
Hebrews 11:3 NKJV

MOMENTS OF REFLECTION

1. What do you fear most? What is the root of your fear? How has it impacted your life?

2. What types of fear (rejection, man, failure, or success) have impacted you? How can you turn those fears into belief and faith for God's promises for you?

3. Have you received prophetic words that have not come to pass? If so, ask the Lord to reveal the timing and give increased insight into the word for this time.

Notes:

THE RISE OF THE OVERCOMER

CHAPTER 5

RESIST AND CONQUER THE LIES

People who resist the lies of Satan will always have the strength and confidence to overcome the evil working against them. Period.

As I think about resisting and conquering Satan's lies, it reminds me of a situation I was in not too long ago. To give you a little history, most of my teenage and adult life I lived as a fearful, insecure, shameful, and misguided individual. I had always been in the background and was very comfortable being there—until one day God decided to abruptly upset my familiar sense of comfort, or, should I say, my comfortable way of life.

TAKE YOUR SEAT

Here's my story that took place in 2012. Even now, I get goosebumps just thinking about it. I was sitting in my usual place at church by the wall on the left side of the building, minding my own business. I never sat toward the front because I didn't want to ever draw attention to myself, even though I had been ordained as a minister the previous year. I felt like I wasn't the type of person to get up and have all eyes on me. However, being shy and insecure ultimately left zero room for me to minister to the congregation. My attitudes and perceptions were blocking me from moving into my calling, but at the time I didn't understand that.

On this particular Sunday, a friend of mine came over and said, "Are you aware of the seat in the front row with your name on it?"

I frantically yelled, "No!"

He explained how the front row had been set apart for the leaders of the ministry. I was freaking out. Up to that point, I had not even seen myself as a leader. I knew I had been ordained to minister, but I certainly didn't think it was going to disrupt my comfort level and cause me to change my physical and spiritual positioning. God had called me to feed His sheep, and I was doing that behind the scenes. No one needed to know about it. Really? So, I declined and stayed where I was.

After my friend informed me about these chairs at the front that were marked for my husband and me, I felt like I was now haunted by them throughout every week. I couldn't go to our regular meetings without thinking about them. As a matter of fact, before or after service I'd slowly pass by the seats just to see if they had changed their minds about the seats being assigned to us. Maybe, just maybe, they had given them to some special people. I was horrified to see that one of the seats still had my name on it. I literally thought to myself, "Why is this happening to me?"

I finally prayed to the Lord and asked Him to help me with the situation. He responded by saying, "Take your seat." At that time, I was filled with so much fear and insecurity that the very thought of sitting on that front row absolutely terrified me. But I knew that I had to obey God. After a couple of weeks had gone by, I finally did it. Frankly, every hidden fear or stronghold within my soul began to manifest, but I still stood in the place where God was calling me to stand. God has performed miracles through that small act of obedience. I've never gone back to the place where I once sat in fear.

Finally, be strong in the Lord and in his mighty power. Put on the full armor of God, so that you can take your stand against the devil's schemes. For our struggle is not against flesh and blood, but against the rulers, against the authorities, against the powers of this dark world and against the spiritual forces of evil in the heavenly realms.

— *Ephesians 6:10-12 NIV*

Know this. We are going to have to stand boldly in our God-given authority and overthrow everything that is working against our kingdom identity or stealing our communion with the Lord. Because here's the real truth: Many times the enemy knows more about our spiritual identity than we do. The enemy knows that when we're doing what God has called us to do, we are at our strongest, greatest, and most effective place. It's where the truth is magnified, and every lie is exposed. It's the place of power and authority, which ultimately becomes the place of victory.

So we must put on our spiritual armor daily and gird our minds with the Word of God. We must recognize that we are in a war every day. We have an opponent who is fighting to bring destruction upon everything that pertains to life and godliness. We must live with this awareness so that we can overcome and completely demolish any stronghold He has in our lives.

Be sober, be vigilant; because your adversary the devil walks about like a roaring lion, seeking whom he may devour.

— *1 Peter 5:8*

Our discernment is also key. We must discern by the Holy Spirit and recognize when the enemy is in our atmosphere. It is vital that we pay attention to how the devil is operating so that we can bring an end to it. We need to be strategic and shrewd in the way we deal with the devil so the Lord's purposes can continue to move forward and be established.

Satan's plans are not always obvious, but God will continually reveal such things to those who have a heart to know His will, discerning both good and evil. Evil is continuously lurking to derail and deter the people of God. Sometimes it comes as discouragement. Other times it comes with unfair treatment or the betrayal by a close friend. Whatever the case, we must see through those types of demonic schemes. They are sent against us to prevent us from successfully advancing and fulfilling our calling and purpose on earth. But with the help of the Almighty, we will overcome every plot or weapon of Satan that wants to hold us back or keep us down.

SHOW UP – WHAT SATAN FEARS MOST

Throw off anything that's holding you back and show up. The light that God has placed in you is the only one that's necessary to change your world. Darkness is only present in the absence of light. So if there is going to be any light in our day, in our time, or in our world, we must show up. We must fight and stand up to Satan, not run away from him.

Years ago, I went to visit a friend in the hospital whom I had been praying for concerning a deadly illness. While I was in her hometown, I thought I'd pay her a visit, although I had already heard that she was feeling much better. When I entered the room, I saw a nurse moving around her bed, charting vital signs and other patient information. She then moved to the other side of the room so that we could enjoy our visit.

As we spoke and updated each other on current events, I praised God for what He was doing in both of our lives. The nurse was able to hear our conversation. To my surprise, she began to cry and receive faith for her personal situation. With tears in her eyes and hope in her heart, she turned to me and said, "You have just restored my faith for my marriage!"

I was amazed. I wasn't praying at the time or even quoting any Scriptures. I wasn't even there to speak with her. I was just there to visit a friend. I was simply having a normal conversation, being who I am. What I began to see that day is that my words are filled with spirit and life because God lives within me! When the Light of All Life was released in that moment, the nurse was able to see something different and cross over from the past captivity of despair and discouragement, stepping right into faith and hope for her future. I just showed up, and the enemy was defeated.

This is what Satan fears. When the light shows up, darkness must flee! When people gain hope, faith, and courage for themselves, they begin to reproduce it for others. This fills the earth with the glory of God and drives away evil!

Once again, hear my words. God is ready to transform lives, but we must show up. He is not looking for spiritual giants; He's looking for vessels. He's seeking those filled with His pure light of love, hope, faith, and courage. He's looking for you! He's the *super* working inside your *natural.*

VICTORY OVER THE LIES OF FEAR

Therefore, let God be God in and through you, and watch Him expose evil as He illuminates everything that pertains to you. Truly, it is that simple. This is how we gain victory over the lies of fear and despair. To live the ascended life of the overcomer, we must face fear and conquer it.

How do you conquer fear? First, the Word of God must

disciple you. His truth spoken not only builds your confidence, it also releases the power of Holy Spirit. Any fear you need to conquer can be dispelled through promises and truths in the Bible.

Second, you must abide in the truth. In the Bible, *abide* is a verb and active. Abiding in Christ is not a feeling or a belief, but something you do. It means *to remain or stay*, and it goes far beyond belief in the Savior. John illustrates this abiding relationship in chapter 15.

> *Abide in Me, and I in you. As the branch cannot bear fruit of itself, unless it abides in the vine, neither can you, unless you abide in Me. I am the vine, you are the branches. He who abides in Me, and I in him, bears much fruit; for without Me you can do nothing.*
>
> — *John 15:4-5*

When we abide with Christ and His truth, it becomes a part of us. There's no striving to be, and there's no pressure to act a certain way. He becomes part of the fabric of our being.

Third, you must press past the chatter of others and the threats of danger to enter a higher perspective. There you intentionally posture yourself to see the salvation of the Lord, receive His favor, and gain His victory—just like Moses did.

> *And Moses said to the people, "Do not be afraid. Stand still, and see the salvation of the LORD, which He will accomplish for you today. For the Egyptians whom you see today, you shall see again no more forever. The LORD will fight for you, and you shall hold your peace."*
>
> — *Exodus 14:13-14*

If you will not allow fear to grip you and just begin to trust God with everything you've got, God will fight for you and establish you in peace. You will be fully liberated, and your enemies will be utterly defeated.

MEDITATION FOR APPLICATION

Set aside 15-30 minutes each day to commune with God. Each day read and meditate on one of the Scriptures listed below. Follow these steps.

1. Go to a quiet place without distraction.

2. Play a praise song and just listen to the words.

3. Ask God to reveal His heart and meaning to you as you read the Scriptures.

4. Write your reflections below or in your journal.

5. Read the Scriptures daily so you receive maximum revelation.

James 4:7 NLT
John 15:4-5 NKJV
Exodus 14:13-14 NKJV
Ephesians 6:10-12 NIV

MOMENTS OF REFLECTION

1. What lies cause fear in your heart? How do they hinder you?

2. What lies of the enemy, whether directly or through people, are you agreeing with? How would your life be different if you stopped agreeing with the lies?

3. Where in your life do you need to *show up* to defeat the enemy? How would life be different if you showed up to defeat the enemy?

Notes:

The Rise of the Overcomer

Chapter 6
Overcome Hurt

The world is always evolving, and trends are always changing. Many people are dealing with the stress and pressures of modern culture. Technology drives society, and the culture seems to have everyone going along for the ride.

Although the world appears to be morphing as we speak, many of us get stuck in a very constricted space of life, giving little room for growth or change. I can safely say that most of this constriction is due to a thin capacity for adaptability and adjustment. Their soul has been shut down from past pain and trauma

When we detect challenges, change, or a new order, our emotional gates close and our doors of trust get locked so we can avoid pain. Every time we are hurt by someone or something, we will remember it, and it marks us. If we don't deal with it, pain becomes embedded within our emotions. It fastens to our minds and communicates with our will. This is huge. Pain can take over and alter everything about us.

Many people, however, feel we should not acknowledge pain because that brings needless attention to it. They believe that focusing on the pain will magnify it and will cause more harm than good. It is ludicrous and dangerous to hold the belief that pain is nothing. Pain doesn't just disappear into thin air if we ignore it. Tell me, where's the logic in that?

Some people believe that we can acknowledge the hurt but should not stay there too long; we should just bury it and move on. I'll go on record and say that's not possible. The hurt already happened, your brain recorded it, and it has already been downloaded into your memory bank as a danger zone. For example, if someone says something that triggers a reaction connected to a place of trauma within, we might react in an unusual manner. That's when we realize the pain of the trauma is not as buried as we had thought. Ignoring buried wounds will cost us in the long run, because we will live life from a place of bondage instead of from a place of freedom and wholeness.

This is why we must look at pain differently. Rather than seeking to ignore pain, we should learn to process it correctly. This will make the difference between a healthy state of mind and an unhealthy state of mind. If we train ourselves to process any form of affliction with a different lens, we won't be captured by the trauma of it. Looking at painful situations in the right context can not only heal us emotionally but it can also heal us mentally and physically. We will obtain the victory instead of the defeat.

My personal experience paints a picture of this. Not long ago, I dealt with one of the most painful times of my life. Suddenly, it seemed my world was severely rocked. I didn't understand why at the time, but in an instant life became very difficult. I had never felt so powerless. It was like Superman being overwhelmed by kryptonite. The only words that I could utter were, "God, help me." It was emotionally crushing. I felt like I was going out of my mind and that I was absolutely nothing. Where did this come from? Rejection.

Roots of rejection began to come up in ways I had never felt before, and I was really being put to the test. My deepest pains sprang up like fountains and caused me a great deal of anguish that heavily weighed on my soul. Now that I have pressed through and come out on the other side of this crisis, I feel compelled to share the hidden dangers and barriers to emotional stability that come from not dealing with such a major force. We must address these things to become the most powerful version of who we are, for ourselves and for those who are around us.

After walking through such gross darkness, I've been able to capture a much brighter light. My experience has caused me to take a longer look at others from a very different perspective. For instance now I see that many who are labeled as rebellious troublemakers are really people who don't or can't alleviate the suffering associated with their past traumatic situation. They act out because their hostile and painful emotional condition speaks louder than anything or anyone else around them. For example, people who are easily offended and seem to wear their feelings on their sleeves often suffer from deep-rooted issues of pain and trauma. Have you ever taken time to see people like this through the lens of personal trauma, or do you avoid them, keeping your distance? They appear to be a nuisance to have to deal with, but the reality is that most of them are not waking up each morning to set a goal to remain angry and offended.

Typically, a situation occurs that touches or triggers a very sensitive, painful area of the soul. An emotional reaction erupts that points to the underlying issue. Husbands and wives know this scenario well. Parents are also familiar with this, and let's not forget co-workers and bosses who know this extremely well. The conversation that follows is all too familiar.

"Are you okay?"

"What's wrong with you?"

"What did I do? Something is clearly wrong."

"I can't say anything right."

"You wear your feelings on your sleeve."

"Here you go again!"

A number of us can bounce back quickly from even the most unpleasant and difficult situations; we don't give a second thought to negativity or unfavorable situations. We don't have the luxury of getting emotionally stuck, so we tend to just breeze on by and keep moving. We get busy with our business and leave other people's comments, opinions, and criticisms behind for them to process. After all, "If they have problems with me, it's their problem, right?"

Well, I've learned that this is not necessarily true. Here's the truth: Those rejections, criticisms, and unwarranted opinions find their place in us whether we embrace them or not. It's no different than walking on the soil. If we step in the dirt with our feet, we will leave an imprint. It's the same with other people's actions or words. If someone steps on our feelings, we will feel it, and it leaves an awful impression, even if we choose to walk away and ignore it. For this reason, we must be willing to make the effort to deal with negative remarks and respond in the right way.

As hurtful as they can be, these uncomfortable opportunities help us gain understanding and grow, instead of deteriorating emotionally by carrying pain and festering wounds for years.

> *Lord, protect me from this evil one! Rescue me from these violent schemes! He concocts his secret strategy to divide and harm others, stirring up trouble one against another. They are known for their sharp rhetoric of poisonous, hateful words.*
>
> *— Psalm 140:1-3 TPT*

Words can be sharp and powerful. They can thrust us forward or beat us down. They can heal our hurts or poison our heart. This is why we pray for the Lord to guard our heart.

THE EFFECTS OF PAIN

When we do not acknowledge our hurt and we allow pain to live in our heart, we become infected with what I call Hurt Disease and Disorder (HDD). This condition of the heart spreads quickly into numerous areas of our life. It alters our relationships and affects our beliefs. It twists our perception, causing us to make wrong choices. It poisons our thoughts, changes our speech, steals our quality of life, and snatches everything good from our well-being. Most dangerous of all, it changes the core of who we are. It's just awful!

When we allow HDD to have a place in our heart, we must identify its characteristics so it can be dismantled and evicted. Many times, we habitually behave in wrong ways and we don't notice or don't understand why we're negatively responding. We must look at and address these behaviors with clear eyes.

Let's take a look at some of the symptoms that come with Hurt Disease and Disorder. Mistrust, suspicion, cynicism, sarcasm, bitterness, dread, lack of faith, lack of relationship, frustration, control, manipulation, isolation, stagnation, criticism, and judgment are some of the most common symptoms. People under the influence of HDD are also more susceptible to arrested development, depression, anxiety, mental disorders, negative cycles, and destructive behaviors.

A familiar saying is that hurting people hurt people. This is very true, but it does not have to be the narrative every time. When we allow ourselves to look beyond external behavior, we'll see that individuals who inflict pain are filled with their own injury, which causes them to ignorantly spew it out on others. Once we become fully cognizant of this cycle of affliction, we can disrupt the HDD cycle by following the Word of God. Instead of receiving bruised feelings, we can offer love, freedom, and transformation to people who are suffering with the torment of painful trauma. Let's look at Joseph in the book of Genesis.

Joseph's brothers hated him because his father favored him. They angrily betrayed him by selling him as a slave to the Midianites. In Egypt, the Midianites sold Joseph to Potiphar, one of Pharaoh's officials, who was the captain of the guard. It was clear that Joseph no longer had control over his own life or any of the circumstances that pertained to him. Can you imagine how painful that must have been?

81

Potiphar recognized that everything Joseph did was successful because God was with him, so he put Joseph in charge of everything he owned. Consequently, Joseph obtained favor with God and men. He never buried himself in bitterness, unforgiveness, self-pity, or resentment. He kept serving and honoring the Lord as he had been taught in his father's house. Soon after his promotion, he was falsely accused by Potiphar's wife and thrown into prison. But even while Joseph was in prison, the Lord was with him. God granted Joseph favor in the eyes of the prison warden, and he was placed in charge of all the other prisoners.

After a turn of events while diligently serving in prison, Joseph was called to interpret Pharaoh's dream. God gave him the interpretation and released the wisdom required to prepare for an impending famine that was coming to the land of Egypt. Pharaoh was amazed at the power and presence of God that rested upon Joseph. He decided to make Joseph the governor of the land and put him in charge of the entire palace and all of Egypt's affairs.

During the famine, Joseph's brothers came to Egypt to buy food because they had heard there was great food supply in Egypt. What they did not know was this had become available because their brother Joseph had faithfully stewarded the land and stored up food for years before the famine ever arrived. Joseph recognized his brothers. He knew that God had brought them to Egypt, so he did not reject them. Instead, he revealed himself to them. The brothers recognized that God was with him, in spite of all their evil plots. God had used all of the pain, rejection, abandonment, and abuse for the good of the people.

> *Then Joseph said to his brothers, "Come close to me." When they had done so, he said, "I am your brother Joseph, the one you sold into Egypt! And*

now, do not be distressed and do not be angry with yourselves for selling me here, because it was to save lives that God sent me ahead of you."

— *Genesis 45:4-5 NIV*

Then his brothers also went and fell down before his face, and they said, "Behold, we are your servants." Joseph said to them, "Do not be afraid, for am I in the place of God? But as for you, you meant evil against me; but God meant it for good, in order to bring it about as it is this day, to save many people alive. Now therefore, do not be afraid; I will provide for you and your little ones."

— *Genesis 50:18-21*

We must see things through a more comprehensive point of view. Pain is not the main thing; it is simply a part of the process. We must embrace and be willing to walk through pain so we can live triumphantly. If we see it as a danger, or something to be avoided, we will magnify it and begin to live in dysfunctional cycles that alter our identity and destiny, as well as our heart.

HURT AND THE CYCLE OF CONTROL

When we are hurt, we may act out our pain by attempting to control others through manipulation, force, or pressure to make them conform and do whatever we wish. We act this way instead of dealing with past trauma where we felt out of control. The cycle of control becomes a coping mechanism that makes us feel a false sense of security, safety, and protection. These controlling behaviors also cover up the pain of the pre-existing wounds, diverting all attention away from our struggle with our own internal pain.

Instead, we need to be led and directed by the Spirit of God. He will not only protect us but He will also reveal what we need to be made whole in every area of our lives. We won't have to control or manipulate others or situations when we know that God is working on our behalf. He will bring increase to our lives and destroy the works of darkness that diminish our quality of life.

Jesus went to the cross so that we as children of God would have full access to the throne of grace. Through this grace we experience God's power, provision, and protection in an unceasing way. He alone is the source of life.

I remember a time my son sent me a picture of a well-known Christian pastor standing beside a very controversial, misguided public figure. I used this opportunity as a teaching moment. I explained to my son that this pastor is still a great pastor to many, and a member of God's family. If God doesn't turn his back on him, then why should we reject others? The pastor had done no wrong by being in this man's company. Like the rest of us, he had been given free will to choose what he believed was right. Those choices would be judged by the One who gave him the freedom to choose, not by mankind.

It is important for each believer to remember these principles as we move throughout life's journey. We must see the body of Christ no differently than our own family. We don't sever ties with blood relatives for making bad choices. So also we should not do it to the family of God if the Holy Spirit has not exposed the workings of Satan among them.

Cancel culture has caused an epidemic of offense to run rampant in our society, but it must not affect the people of God. We operate by the laws of God, which are a higher level of principles and standards that are rooted in God's righteousness and truth. Life will continue to sporadically release pain, hurt, and disappointment, but when we know how to respond well in those moments, we can move with grace to overcome. That grace is given to lead us into triumph, moment by moment.

When we are not taught how to properly navigate through these hurts, they can cripple us. If we become aware of what impacts our souls and how that influences us, we can be more active and intentional in dealing with unresolved hurt, which can poison our hearts and minds.

PROCESS PAIN IN THE RIGHT WAY

Pain hurts. There's just no other way to say it. Whether I stump my toe, hit my elbow, or cut my finger, it doesn't feel good, and I never get used to it. Internal pain is no different. When someone lies to us, betrays us, or cheats on us, it hurts deeply. It's excruciatingly painful and must be acknowledged for any healing to take place.

In the natural sense, certain physical wounds need special attention. Doctors use sutures so that a severe wound can heal properly. Internal wounds need special attention too; don't be fooled by what isn't visible. If we have been wounded, symptoms or reactions that show will point us to a root cause. This is why we shouldn't be quick to judge people by their actions. Identifying the source of the trauma gives us the power to change the condition. If we are not able to recognize the issue at hand, we can never assume that we can eliminate it.

Awareness positions and empowers us to understand what is needed to overcome trauma and pursue a new trajectory for the future. When we can identify the source, the root cause of trauma, we can respond with godly intentionality to see it healed, and we can begin to live in a place of wholeness and peace.

Let's look at this descriptive verse that addresses the confronting of trauma to see joy on the other side. Jesus endured the cross for the joy set before Him.

Looking unto Jesus, the author and finisher of our faith, who for the joy that was set before Him endured the cross, despising the shame, and has sat down at the right hand of the throne of God.

— Hebrews 12:2

Does that mean Jesus acted as if there was no cross? No, not at all. It means that He saw that experience on the cross as the only way to get to the great joy that was set before Him. He endured the suffering so the Father's covenant plan for the salvation of mankind could be fulfilled. What a victory!

Jesus' pain is no different than when a woman gives birth. Think about it. She must fix her mind on the blessing of the small, fragile person passing through her womb more than the labor, suffering, and discomfort she will endure throughout the process. However, for the joy that is set before her, she endures. In many cases, because the joy is so much more rewarding than the pain, women will endure the suffering over and over again as they grow their families by bringing more children into the world.

When we do not process hurt, betrayal, abandonment, or rejection correctly, we become ensnared by them, and all those painful experiences rule our lives. Our feelings, thoughts, and beliefs become trapped in dark spaces of our souls, and they ultimately cause us to live in habitual and daily misery, anger, bitterness, confusion, frustration, and sometimes depression. How do we process pain effectively? The only way we can possibly respond in the right way to anything that happens in this life is by instructions for each situation from God's Word.

APPLY THE WORD TO PAIN

The Bible has prescriptions for hurtful situations. It teaches us how to respond in the midst of heartache and trouble inflicted by others. Let's look at some of them.

> *If another believer sins against you, go privately and point out the offense. If the other person listens and confesses it, you have won that person back.*
>
> — *Matthew 18:15 NLT*

> *Even if my father and mother abandon me, the LORD will hold me close.*
>
> — *Pslam 27:10 NLT*

> *But I say, love your enemies! Pray for those who persecute you!*
>
> — *Matthew 5:44 NLT*

> *If you forgive those who sin against you, your heavenly Father will forgive you. But if you refuse to forgive others, your Father will not forgive your sins.*
>
> — *Matthew 6:14-15 NLT*

When you are on the way to court with your adversary,
settle your differences quickly.

— Matthew 5:25 NLT

And "don't sin by letting anger control you." Don't
let the sun go down while you are still angry.

— Ephesians 4:26 NLT

Get rid of all bitterness, rage, anger, harsh words, and
slander, as well as all types of evil behavior. Instead,
be kind to each other, tenderhearted, forgiving one
another, just as God through Christ has forgiven you.

— Ephesians 4:31-32 NLT

These are just some of the practical prescriptions given to overcome hurtful and uncomfortable situations. God has given us everything we need to be victorious. This is what makes us more than conquerors. We are powerful beyond measure because Almighty God has given us the power to overcome any troublesome or painful situation that we deal with in this earthly life.

Who shall separate us from the love of Christ? Shall
tribulation, or distress, or persecution, or famine, or
nakedness, or peril, or sword? As it is written:
"For Your sake we are killed all day long;
We are accounted as sheep for the slaughter."
Yet in all these things we are more than conquerors
through Him who loved us.

— Romans 8:35-37

OVERCOMING CHURCH HURT

Church hurt is a common hot topic in modern society. People describe this as rejection, betrayal, abuse, or offense caused by people in the church or affiliated with religious institutions. Many have said that these wounds are much more hurtful because these things are inflicted by those who are supposed to walk in Christ-like character, displaying greater levels of love, support, and encouragement than the world.

When I first became a Christian, I was a twenty-four-year-old single mom of twin girls. I was on fire for the Lord and could not wait to get to church on most days. God began to cleanse my heart and restore my life immediately. He wasted no time! I experienced so many breakthroughs and miracles during that time, it was easy for me to believe how much God loved me. He poured out His love in every area of my life.

Unfortunately, some people in my church did not feel the same as God did. All they could see was a young unwed mother who had done very bad things to get herself into a shameful situation. They looked at me as if I reeked with sin. They talked about me to my face and behind my back. I felt kind of like Hester Prynne, who had to endure public humiliation for committing adultery in the best-selling novel the *Scarlet Letter.*

It was a very ugly situation, and it got worse once I started dating my husband, who happened to be a promising and gifted college student with no children at all. Thankfully, I was so captivated by the grace and love of God that it did not make me run away. I stayed at this particular church so that I would learn to know God more and grow in my relationship with Him. My desperate heart was always fixed on God, not people, because I needed God to transform my heart and change my life. I was always very aware of my need for Him. I believe this is the reason why the hurt did not remain in my soul. The more I encountered the Lord, the more I overcame the fiery, weaponized words that were hurled at me out of people's ignorance. My experiences with God completely overshadowed all the gossip, judgment, and backbiting that took place around me.

Not long after my husband and I were married, God led us to a different Christian congregation. I wish I could say it got easier but, truthfully, it did not. We encountered very different types of grief and trouble from very different types of people, but it was still church hurt.

Over the years, I have spent countless hours in prayer and counseling. However, after so many different scenarios with so many different people, I can only conclude one thing: Church people are just as human as other human beings. They are people who are still finding their way to the cross of Christ and receiving the same mercy and grace that God gives to all men. They are not better or worse than people in the world. Their titles and positions do not make them any less human. They are just people, people who are given to God.

We should apply the same godly principles and responses to those who hurt or betray us within the church as we do for those in the workplace or at the supermarket. We must forgive them the same as we forgive all who trespass against us. As we pray for their brokenness to be healed, God will reward us with healing in our own hearts. We will reap exactly what we sow into the lives of others.

And the King will say, "I tell you the truth, when you did it to one of the least of these my brothers and sisters, you were doing it to me!"

— Matthew 25:40 NLT

What we do for our sisters and brothers, we do to Him. It's as simple as that. Jesus loves them just as much as He loves us. He wants to bless them and make them whole in every way.

ACTION TO OVERCOME HURT

You must learn to take action—without taking offense—to overcome the effects of hurt. The impact of personal pain will not magically disappear without taking intentional steps forward that promote healing and growth. We can profit physically, mentally, and emotionally from trials when we approach them the right way. Here's what James says in the New Testament:

> *My brethren, count it all joy when you fall into various trials, knowing that the testing of your faith produces patience. But let patience have its perfect work, that you may be perfect and complete, lacking nothing. If any of you lacks wisdom, let him ask of God, who gives to all liberally and without reproach, and it will be given to him. But let him ask in faith, with no doubting, for he who doubts is like a wave of the sea driven and tossed by the wind. For let not that man suppose that he will receive anything from the Lord; he is a double-minded man, unstable in all his ways.*
>
> *— James 1:2-8*

As impossible as it may seem, counting the tough times in our life as fodder for our growth allows us to count it all for joy. God grows us this way so that we can accomplish the Kingdom purposes that He has planned for our life. We will not only conquer the pain but also flourish in fulfilling our purpose and personal goals.

MEDITATION FOR APPLICATION

Set aside 15-30 minutes each day to commune with God. Each day read and meditate on one of the Scriptures listed below. Follow these steps.

1. Go to a quiet place without distraction.

2. Play a praise song and just listen to the words.

3. Ask God to reveal His heart and meaning to you as you read the Scriptures.

4. Write your reflections below or in your journal.

5. Read the Scriptures daily so you receive maximum revelation.

Matthew 18:15 NLT
Ephesians 4:26 NLT
Matthew 6:14 NLT

MOMENTS OF REFLECTION

1. Examine your heart. What hurts have you harbored? How has that impacted the joy and fullness of your life?

2. Who do you need to forgive? Who do you need to receive forgiveness from to move forward, including other people and/ or the Lord?

3. What are the actions you will take to overcome the pain of the past?

Notes:

THE RISE OF THE OVERCOMER

CHAPTER 7
OVERCOME PRIDE

Merriam-Webster's dictionary defines pride in different ways, but the definition I will address is the one that's common to most of us. This dictionary defines it as follows: "Pride (n.):1. too high an opinion of one's own ability or worth; 2. reasonable self-esteem: confidence and satisfaction in oneself."

This definition indicates that our pride can be healthy or unhealthy. It can be beneficial or destructive, depending on the position we take and the posture of our heart. Healthy self-esteem and confidence enable us to flourish and succeed. Healthy self-esteem can help us to be productive, balanced, and clear-thinking when managing our personal affairs, relationships, and responsibilities. We have better relationships, healthier self-awareness, and greater productivity.

Here are some of the most common characteristics and signs of healthy self-esteem. We are humble, helpful, and considerate because we have nothing to prove to others. We also have the attitude of a team-player, decision-maker, or solutionist because we want to keep things moving forward and working properly to meet the need or accomplish specific goals. We can put our feelings aside and look deeper into a situation to gain a larger perspective. We can bridle our emotions and attitudes so we are more effective and gain a higher vantage point.

On the other hand, unhealthy pride keeps us from manifesting the greatness of who God created us to be. It's the form of pride that seats us higher than we ought to be, which is higher than the wisdom of God.

God has given me grace to speak a warning about pride. I would ask each of you to be emptied of self-promotion and not create a false image of your importance. Instead, honestly assess your worth by using your God-given faith as the standard of measurement, and then you will see your true value with an appropriate self-esteem.

— *Romans 12:3 TPT*

The wording that Paul uses in this verse reveals the intensity of the subject matter. He basically says, "Consider this to be a warning." Wow. This language creates and speaks of a significant, sobering moment. It calls us to attention and stills us enough to hear the warning that is coming forth. This is a major key for avoiding pitfalls.

God delivers the warning by giving instruction. He says that we are to empty ourselves of self-promotion and the deception of our lofty self-image or self-worth. He demands that we honestly assess our worth according to the measure of faith given by God. Any time we assess ourselves outside of God's wisdom and provision, we deceive ourselves.

Pride can create destructive behaviors that lead to negative consequences. Every one of these behaviors is subject to change once it is identified. Some of these behaviors and their consequences are listed here.

- Arrogance leads to offense and destruction.
- Egotism leads to isolation by driving others away.
- Haughtiness leads to a future fall.
- Manipulation leads to forms of control.
- Possessiveness leads to lack of inner peace.

- Emotional insecurity leads to forms of control.
- Criticism leads to internal blindness.
- Judgment leads to lack of personal freedom.
- Envy or jealousy leads to mental torment.
- Brokenness leads to a broken perspective.
- Self-centeredness leads to mental imprisonment.
- Self-preservation leads to skewed vision.
- Self-righteousness leads to evil behavior.
- Selfishness leads to judgment.
- An independent spirit leads to broken relationships.
- Isolation leads to arrested development.
- Withdrawal leads to mental torment.
- Perfectionism leads to lack of peace and love.
- Constant striving leads to a form of accomplishment.
- Unhealthy competition leads to great insecurity.

Unhealthy pride leads to consequences because it is rooted in self-reliance and human ability rather than reliance on God and all that He is. Pride results in a divided heart, which gives the enemy license to wreak havoc.

When our hearts are divided between God and any idols, which can be our pride, we are not completely given to either party. As Elijah stated in 1 Kings,

> *And Elijah came to all the people, and said, "How long will you falter between two opinions? If the LORD is God, follow Him; but if Baal, follow him." But the people answered him not a word.*

> — *1 Kings 18:21*

PRIDE THAT BINDS THE MIND

Not too long ago, I was up at 3:00 a.m. praying, and the Lord began to speak to me. He showed me a vision of a plastic belt-looking object wrapped around most people's brains that kept them from moving in the way He created them to move. He said this had been placed there by false ideologies and wrong impartations. He said this thing that I was seeing around their brains was squeezing out all hope, life, and belief, leaving them empty with nothing but a sense of helplessness, death, unbelief, and disbelief. When I went to bed it was 4:44 a.m., which was a number I had been seeing all weekend.

I felt compelled to share this experience with a friend, someone I trusted. After talking with my dear friend, I was led to 2 Corinthians 4:4 where it says the god of this world blinded the minds of those who did not believe. I knew the Lord was still highlighting our thinking. He was saying our thinking must make a shift for us to see our future. We will have to see how to move and advance in a new way.

Whose minds the god of this age has blinded, who do not believe, lest the light of the gospel of the glory of Christ, who is the image of God, should shine on them.

— 2 Corinthians 4:4

I also prayed for a family member who was having a personal issue. God showed me that, for her issue to be resolved, her perception must change. She needed to humble herself to see the situation clearly from God's perspective so that necessary breakthroughs would begin to unfold. When she could see as He sees, then she could move forward with knowledge and understanding.

This is the dilemma many are currently facing. People are praying, fasting, and decreeing, along with sowing and going, yet they have not aligned their thinking with the mind of Christ. As a result, people have not seen their brothers and sisters through the eyes of God. Others have not seen their assignments, missions, and callings correctly because they view their lives from an earthly perspective. This viewpoint has skewed their thinking because they are operating from their natural minds.

We must be willing to see beyond our normal perceptions and recognize when we are stuck in the same cycle that God showed me during my 3:00 a.m. prayer time. We cannot afford to remain stuck in what we have always done or to allow the opinions and beliefs of others to frame our way of living.

God is calling for humility so He can reveal the plan He has for us. He wants to breathe on us so we can receive the power to go where He is sending us. He breathed on Jesus to give Him power, then He sent Him into the wilderness. He wants us to get unstuck. God is going to give us the ability to interpret the times and seasons so that we can move accurately with Him. When we get free in our thinking and break out of old cycles, God is going to give us the gift of breakthrough miracles. God is going to deliver us from the captivity of the mind and grant us the ability to do things we have never thought were possible. Strongholds will break off our mind and fall completely away from us, no longer to be found. We can bring down demonic structures in a day.

PRIDE AND OUR THINKING

If we have pride limiting our thinking processes, the Lord cannot lead us out of old cycles and habits that keep us stuck. Our ways of thinking will box us in and limit us from receiving the rewards that God has set aside for us. God gives rewards for obedience, diligence, and faithfulness, but our intellect will cause us to try to gain an illegitimate prize by going outside the boundaries of blessing.

Let's look at intellectualism. Intellectualism is not our friend when it comes to God matters. It can act more as our enemy if we're not careful. Intellectualism causes us to depend on our own thinking rather than relying on Holy Spirit for guidance and understanding. This dysfunctional form of self-reliance causes a chasm or separation from the presence and provision of God.

> *Beware, brethren, lest there be in any of you an evil heart of unbelief in departing from the living God.*
>
> — *Hebrews 3:12*

Education is intended to better equip us in our service to the Lord and others. It should never be the thing that creates another form of bondage, where we are puffed up with knowledge but separated from our true purpose. This leads us into idolatry and builds strongholds in the soul. These demonic strongholds are established through human desire and self-will. This idolatry of the human mind creates a curse.

> *Cursed is the man who trusts in man*
> *And makes flesh his strength,*
> *Whose heart departs from the LORD.*
> *For he shall be like a shrub in the desert,*
> *And shall not see when good comes,*
> *But shall inhabit the parched places in the wilderness,*
> *In a salt land which is not inhabited.*
>
> — *Jeremiah 17:5-6*

The Scripture above describes a person who trusts in himself or others more than the God who made him. Unfortunately, he will inherit a curse instead of a blessing because his heart cannot see things in a straightforward manner. Instead, he is full of cunning deceit and is ever seeking to overdo others.

> *The heart is deceitful above all things,*
> *And desperately wicked;*
> *Who can know it?*
> *I, the LORD, search the heart,*
> *I test the mind,*
> *Even to give every man according to his ways,*
> *According to the fruit of his doings.*

— *Jeremiah 17:9-10*

The destructive pathways of humanism, intellectualism, and rationalism are shown below, from left to right.

Humanism →	Antichrist→	Seduction, tolerance, regression
Intellectualism→	Mind idolatry→	Cycles of lies and deception (conformity, leniency)
Rationalism→	Logic of this world →	Whoredom

Satan produces counterfeits and substitutes that mimic the truth of God. This is why we cannot easily detect what's really operating within. Normally these negative results aren't evident until the consequences appear.

Your heart became proud

on account of your beauty,
and you corrupted your wisdom
because of your splendor.
So I threw you to the earth;
I made a spectacle of you before kings.
By your many sins and dishonest trade
you have desecrated your sanctuaries.
So I made a fire come out from you,
and it consumed you,
and I reduced you to ashes on the ground
in the sight of all who were watching.
All the nations who knew you
are appalled at you;
you have come to a horrible end
and will be no more.

— Ezekiel 28:17-19 NIV

HARMFUL CYCLES OF PRIDE

The main consequence of unhealthy pride is the curse it creates. Pride thrusts us into an order, so we remain in cycles of loss, lack, and restriction. These cycles keep us from advancing and prospering as God intended. Pride gives Satan jurisdiction over our affairs and authorizes him to rule in any situation we are in.

In the book of Judges, we can clearly see the cycles of pride and curses the nation experienced because they were stubborn and rebellious people who saw no need to change until they encountered hardship. They never realized that they needed God as more than a helper who rescues them in times of trouble. God mercifully sent them a deliverer time after time. After they were delivered, they again turned to worship other gods. Then their enemies would appear yet again and bring destruction to their land. The God of Israel repeatedly showed mercy and rescued them by sending another deliverer. This cycle of pride and rebellion kept them from living the life of blessing that God desired for them.

A few weeks ago, I was having a conversation with a friend and God began to show her something spiritually. She saw that a great number of people were going in cycles. She asked the Lord, "Why can't they see they are going in cycles?"

The Lord replied, "Because they are hung up."

She told me that she had attempted to explain to them that there was a pattern or cycle happening, but they couldn't even receive what she was speaking. I told her that they couldn't hear what she was saying because they were hung up in their own thought patterns. They had an emotional attachment to something that caused internal blindness, emotional reticence, and overwhelming anxiety. They didn't want to face the anxiety or discomfort of stepping outside of that cycle and putting their full trust in God. What was happening was the same thing that I had seen in the vision in my early-morning prayer time.

Many times, we get caught up in someone else's cycle. This is just as severe. Our stubbornness and resistance to God's ways lead everyone connected to us in the wrong direction. Pride causes us to get hung up or entrapped.

Every time I think of the term *hung up* in the literal sense, it reminds me of King David's son Absalom. Absalom was David's rebellious son who perceived in his own mind that he could do a better job at being king than David. His pride led him to organize a campaign against his own father so that he could take control of the kingdom. Someone told David that his son had become so evil that he had organized a raid to bring David down and take his throne. David sent his army after Absalom to arrest him and bring him back unharmed. While fleeing from his pursuers, Absalom's hair got caught in a tree that left him dangling from a tree branch. When David's commander saw Absalom dangling from the tree, he pierced his heart with three daggers and killed him.

His hair represents his heart. Because he was not willing to see differently and change his attitude, he got hung up and destroyed. Many of us experience the same thing. We wrestle with internal struggles that keep us hung up and block the blessings that God has for us. We continue to believe and operate according to our own desires and our own expectations that have nothing to do with God's will and predestined plan for us.

OVERCOMING THE PRIDE OF CRITICISM AND JUDGMENT

Criticism and judgment are elements of pride that originate in an internal place of dissatisfaction and brokenness. However, the human reaction to internal dissatisfaction is not to look within but to look outwardly at someone or something else. Our internal dissatisfaction begins to measure other people and external situations with approval or disapproval. We must always be aware that, since internal brokenness gives us a broken perspective, we never see things in a whole way until healing occurs on the inside.

Criticism and judgment come from broken people who have deemed themselves to have a higher perspective or position. But remember, Paul warns in the book of Romans to not think more highly of ourselves than we ought to. When we criticize others, we find fault with them instead of finding good. We see a moment to point out failure and weakness, instead of seeing the opportunity to bless, encourage, support, or help. This produces conflict, conformity, comparison, competition, low self-esteem, and a lack of creativity and freedom. It cuts off the joys of life and does not allow room for love to be expressed.

The best way to overcome these harsh attitudes is to allow the love and mercy of God to flood our heart. We must be willing to receive love and kindness from others as well. This will melt the hardness in our heart and heal the woundedness of the past. It will reset our perspective and cause us to see differently. Then we will be able to edify and encourage others, instead of peering in judgment and finding fault.

OVERCOMING RELIGIOUS PRIDE

Religious pride is a haughty attitude that operates by self-righteous beliefs, religious duty, and performance. When we have religious pride, we attempt to gain satisfaction, approval, acceptance, or affirmation through good works, devotion, and achievement. We rarely like to appear weak or wrong, and we are inclined to criticize others who don't meet our standards.

We must remember that Jesus Christ is the Head of the Body. What He says is right is right, and what He says is wrong is wrong. He does not condemn others, nor should we. We cannot take His position and make others feel condemned. As a matter of fact, He provides a way for them to come into a new place of healing, freedom, and restoration. We should always seek to do the same.

Jesus responded vehemently to the people who tried to accuse the woman who was caught in adultery and said, "He who is without sin, cast the first stone" (see John 8:7). They all began to drop their stones because no one could claim to be without sin. This is why we should faithfully make it a practice to always examine our own selves and let God judge others.

The first message of the New Testament church came through the mouth of John the Baptist. It was the foundation of our relationship with God and all men. John declared, "Repent, for the Kingdom of God is here!" (see Matthew 3:2). This was the announcement of God's order and government coming into the earth realm and dwelling among men.

One of the main ways we fall into prideful attitudes happens when we do not acknowledge our wrongful behaviors or sinful ways of living. We seem to be afraid to admit when we are wrong or want to escape the shame of being in error. This too is a form of pride because we must be humble to receive guidance or correction. This is why repentance is necessary; it is the key to moving forward in the right way. Repentance happens when we purposefully acknowledge our wrong, decide to align with God's way, and deliberately move in a different direction.

Pride is a stumbling block that keeps us from confessing our faults and moving past them. It prevents advancement and keeps us stuck in the confines of our own thoughts. If we confess our sin, we will be healed and able to experience a level of freedom. We will be set free to receive love in a new way and prosper. The flesh will always be at war with the ways of God, but we must choose humility to go the way of victory.

Repentance also involves receiving the mind and heart of God. The people who follow the Lord's ways must embrace His heart. The truth of God does not allow room for pride. When we know the heart of God, it transforms our heart and broadens our perspective. We no longer see from an earthly place, but through the eyes of Abba God. Our minds are renewed by the Spirit of Truth and through the meditation of His holy Word.

Another danger of pride is that it keeps us in mental, spiritual, and emotional bondage. It limits our vision and restricts us from knowing what God has in store for us, outside of the way we envision things to be. So why settle for only a house if God wants to give us the world? Why settle for shepherding sheep if God wants us to shepherd a nation? We must be willing to repent and renew our mind so that we can enter God's perfect plan.

GOD'S THOUGHTS AND WISDOM ABOVE OUR THOUGHTS

We must clear the room in our hearts to hear all of God's thoughts and all of the knowledge He wants to communicate to us for His glory to be made known.

> *Jesus said to him, "You shall love the LORD your God with all your heart, with all your soul, and with all your mind." This is the first and great commandment.*

— Matthew 22:37-38

That word *commandment* is a very powerful word. It says, "Do this." When we look at the conversation Jesus was having with this man, we need to understand that definition when Jesus answered his question. He wasn't giving His opinion or suggesting something that could be applicable. No, not at all. He was telling him the truth of God's will. This is what is required and desired from God, so do it.

Remember, love is an action word, so God wants us to be willing to love with all of our mind. That means we must give Him first place in our minds and allow Him to be seated in that space. He gets to do and reveal whatever He wants to in that space. We must make room for Him there. It's not our thoughts and His thoughts mingling together.

We must be honest with Him and say, "I receive Your thoughts above my own because your thoughts are higher. I am willing to love You with all of my mind. Have Your way in me." This is how we love the Lord with our minds.

For the foolishness of God is wiser than human wisdom, and the weakness of God is stronger than human strength.

— 1 Corinthians 1:25 NIV

We already know that God's thoughts are higher than our thoughts, but the Bible also says that the foolishness of God is wiser than any wisdom of man. For this reason, we must practice leaning into God more than allowing ourselves to be moved or directed by circumstances.

The Lord never meant for us to live without His omniscient wisdom. We were predestined to abide with Him and live a blessed life. God's mercy has already gone before us and prepared a place of blessing for each of us to dwell in. One of the many blessings is the spirit of wisdom and revelation. This gift brings understanding and allows us to move rightly according to God's purposes.

I have not stopped thanking God for you. I pray for you constantly, asking God, the glorious Father of our Lord Jesus Christ, to give you spiritual wisdom and insight so that you might grow in your knowledge of God.

— Ephesians 1:16-17 NLT

Throughout the Bible we are continually urged to not turn away from God's commands. God's wisdom must be applied to unlock the mysteries pertaining to life and our identity. It's His revealed knowledge that gives us the truth about who we are and why we are in this world. This is not simply for our benefit but it's also for the well-being of our families, communities, and nations. We are to be in constant communion with the Holy Spirit to establish God's divine plan to release the Kingdom of Heaven here on Earth.

> *To the twelve tribes which are scattered abroad. If any of you lacks wisdom, let him ask of God, who gives to all liberally and without reproach, and it will be given to him.*
>
> — *James 1:1,5*

In the above Scripture, James the apostle is speaking prophetically. The Lord knows we cannot do it without Him, and sometimes we get so immersed in the systems of the world that we begin to operate from that dimension while trying to fulfill God's plan. Even Jesus, the Son of God, needed Holy Spirit to come and impart life to Him, so that He could do the works that God had sent Him to do. Jesus received the Holy Spirit so he could walk victoriously by the Spirit.

> *The Holy Spirit, in bodily form, descended on him like a dove. And a voice from heaven said, "You are my dearly loved Son, and you bring me great joy."*
>
> — *Luke 3:22 NLT*

He needed Holy Spirit to reveal the truth of past, present, and future so He could be fruitful in every way. By intimately knowing who God is and the power of His Spirit, we receive an impartation and become more like Him. We are made strong, bold, and courageous. We are empowered to love unconditionally and sacrificially. We are transformed into His humble servants and brave warriors. When we leave pride behind, pray, and ask for God's wisdom, we will receive everything we need by prophetic revelation to change the world.

PRIDE SOLUTIONS

The cross is the only way to get rid of pride. The cross of Christ reminds us of the continual sacrifice that we must make. Modern churches live by convenience, but our worship must have a sacrifice for it to be acceptable to the Lord.

> *I beseech you therefore, brethren, by the mercies of God, that you present your bodies a living sacrifice, holy, acceptable to God, which is your reasonable service.*

> *— Romans 12:1*

Many people don't understand why we do not see the power of God like they did in the New Testament. Well, the answer is very simple: We have changed the narrative. Jesus told us specifically what to do and how to live, but we pridefully do what we feel or think is right, instead of what God says is right.

We are directed by God to deny our flesh daily. This compels us to do what He says to remain on His side, the side of abundant life and blessing. Everything done outside of His will is pride, which leads to destruction.

> *Then He said to them all, "If anyone desires to come after Me, let him deny himself, and take up his cross daily, and follow Me.*

> *— Luke 9:23*

This is why it becomes extremely important for us to demonstrate our faith in a godly and righteous manner. The younger generation must know His ways, not ours, and stand upon His words, not man's. They must understand the sacrifice it takes to see the purposes of God established in their generation. They must know that everyone is called to humble themselves and take up their cross to truly follow Him. As we do this, we should seek the Lord and ask, "Why did You put me on this planet? Who am I according to Your plan? How am I to establish it?"

FATHER KNOWS BEST

Whose principles do we live by—God's or our own—when it comes to who deserves forgiveness, who deserves the blessing, who deserves the position or promotion, who deserves justice or judgment? God, the Father of creation, bestows good gifts to His children simply because He loves us. He is love, and everything He sees and does is from a heart of love. Grace is infinitely pouring into our lives solely because He has set His loving desire upon us. As we step into our grace-filled lives daily, we dare not think that we deserve anything that has been freely given to us or that someone else should earn the blessings that our Father longs to release into our lives.

The nature of God will be found in the children of God. They will carry His fragrance and essence. They'll love like He loves and give as He gives from a pure heart, without any form of pride tainting or distorting the visible expression of God.

MEDITATION FOR APPLICATION

Set aside 15-30 minutes each day to commune with God. Each day read and meditate on one of the Scriptures listed below. Follow these steps.

1. Go to a quiet place without distraction.

2. Play a praise song and just listen to the words.

3. Ask God to reveal His heart and meaning to you as you read the Scriptures.

4. Write your reflections below or in your journal.

5. Read the Scriptures daily so you receive maximum revelation.

1 Corinthians 1:25 NIV
Luke 3:22 NLT
James 1:5 NKJV

MOMENTS OF REFLECTION

1. Where in life do you struggle with pride issues? How has this impacted your life?

2. How have humanism, intellectualism, and rationalism impacted your life? What are their sources? How have they impacted your family?

3. How well do you apply God's wisdom to your life rather than your own logic? What can you do to recognize His wisdom as higher than your thoughts?

Notes:

The Rise of the Overcomer

Chapter 8
Overcome Limitations and Prosper

The Lord greatly wants us to prosper, but we must decide to receive and establish this belief. So I give you this charge today! Dare to establish a mindset that overcomes every limitation that you have placed upon yourself. Expect to prosper.

A mentality gives the capacity and capability to receive and produce according to one's view and outlook. It is easily adjustable and adaptable, and it is greatly susceptible. In other words, if the view changes, the mind changes. We can see red or we can see blue at any given moment, because it's naturally neutral.

A mindset is a person's fixed or established way of seeing and believing, consisting of attitudes and fundamental beliefs. Mindsets play an important role in how we process and respond to life's uncertainties, circumstances, and challenges. As we know, many factors influence our individual mindset, like our upbringing, past traumas, close friends and family, culture, and core values.

Mindsets can be liberating and positive or they can be debilitating and negative. What we establish, we will live. In any case, mindsets can significantly impact our outcome by determining who we are, what we think, and how we react and proceed.

RELIGION

Beloved friends, what should be our proper response to God's marvelous mercies? To surrender yourselves to God to be his sacred, living sacrifices. And live in holiness, experiencing all that delights his heart. For this becomes your genuine expression of worship. Stop imitating the ideals and opinions of the culture around you, but be inwardly transformed by the Holy Spirit through a total reformation of how you think. This will empower you to discern God's will as you live a beautiful life, satisfying and perfect in his eyes.

— Romans 12:1-2 TPT

Let's take a look in the Gospel of John (see chapter 5) at the man at the pool of Bethesda who had been in his lame condition for a very long time. Jesus asked him, "Do you want to be made whole?" *Whole* means *increase.* So Jesus was asking, "Do you want to flourish and increase?" The man had been in his condition for thirty-eight years.

Jesus addressed his desire, not his physical condition. He was asking, "Do you want to be whole?" The Lord wanted to find out if the man was convinced that he was already made whole. This indicates that something was already accomplished.

Among the many sick people lying there was a man who had been disabled for thirty-eight years. When Jesus saw him lying there, he knew that the man had been crippled for a long time. Jesus said to him, "Do you truly long to be well?"

— John 5:5-6 TPT

When James and I were ministering in a small village of Africa one time, there came a point where I had to excuse myself from the service for a moment to regain a sense of God's presence. There was so much religious activity going on during the service that I had to leave to find the place where I could reconnect and get back into fellowship with the Lord. People were so set in their religious mindsets that they could not see past them to enter into the presence of God and watch Him move.

To me, this is like the man at the pool of Bethesda, who couldn't see beyond his familiar, religious belief. He thought the only way he could be healed was through the established, traditional process. Then the Son of the living God asked him if he wanted to be healed. Jesus broke the mold and told him, "Stand up, pick up your sleeping mat, and you will walk."

God does not want us to stay stuck in our confidence in religious processes and belief systems, especially if they keep us from accomplishing His purposes. Are we telling God, like the man at Bethesda, what our obstacles are? We must not let our religion keep us from hearing God's promises and moving forward with His plan for our life.

> *Beloved, I wish above all things that thou mayest prosper and be in health, even as thy soul prospereth.*

> — *3 John 1:2 KJV*

Do you hear His passionate desire for you in this verse? How can you not? Above all things He desires for you to prosper and be in health. What He is saying here is, "I am fully committed to seeing this happen in your life. There is no greater purpose in My heart than to see you prosper and be in health, just as your soul prospers."

In this passage, the Greek word for *health* means *to have complete health.* The connotation is to be well in the body, to be uncorrupt and true in doctrine, to be safe and sound, and to be whole in every way. In addition to this, the Greek word for

117

prosper means *to have help and great success.*

We must be able to see the beautiful plan He has for us so the pain of yesterday can be released. We must receive the power of His love so the strongholds of rejection and victimization can be torn down. And we must know in our heart that God is here to help us and prosper us as we decide to change our way of thinking and leave the past behind.

TRADITIONS OF MEN

Beware lest any man spoil you through philosophy and vain deceit, after the tradition of men, after the rudiments of the world, and not after Christ.

— *Colossians 2:8 KJV*

Our earthly traditions can be limiting and therefore prevent us from prospering the way God wants us to. For example, in the world of business we might be taught to exalt ourselves, to build a legacy that is focused on what we want. This may build vain deceit and take us totally off track from God's plans. When we put Him, His promises, and His plans first, we set the groundwork to prosper in the way He wants us to.

CARNALITY

"If it feels good, do it" is an adage that was popular in American culture in the 1960s and 1970s. It refers to attending to our physical human desires. While God wants our needs to be met, which includes physical needs, sometimes we go after what will make us feel good in the moment, but in the long term it will become a limitation.

Imagine the person who ends the stressful workday feeling

118

unappreciated. He or she feels better by going home and rudely barking orders at their family members. In the short term it may feel good, but in the long term it creates an environment of limitation and hostility, which prevents the person's soul from prospering in the way that God ordained. This is what carnality does. Carnality gives momentary gratification to the natural desires of men, but it never satisfies the need or establishes the cycle of blessing that God intends for each of us.

POVERTY

A poverty mindset plagues many people, even in the church. Some of this comes from old religious traditions or from people whining and complaining, talking too much about their state of poverty. Poverty comes in many forms. It could be lack of financial resources, constant sickness, or poor relationships. In any case, this is not what God wants for people. Part of the problem is we are trying to do things our own way and using our own power to get it done. This causes us to fall short of achieving the blessing of prosperity.

Let's see what the Scripture says:

> *And you shall remember the LORD your God, for it is He who gives you power to get wealth, that He may establish His covenant which He swore to your fathers, as it is this day.*

> — *Deuteronomy 8:18*

Notice that the Lord gives us the power to create and obtain wealth. So why do we run off and try to do things our own way? Or why do we shake our fist at God and blame Him for our lack of finances, relationships, or any other part of wealth? Could it be that we didn't really seek His power, wisdom, and ability in the first place? Perhaps we are not in a place of communion and intimacy with God so that we can hear what He wants us to do.

When we are prepared to do something profitable, we must always ask ourselves, "Is this a good idea or a God idea?" His power gives us power to do everything we need to do. Is God able to help me become a lawyer, professional artist, entrepreneur, etc.? The answer is one hundred percent "yes," and it is always "yes"! Seek the Lord continually and He will give you the necessary power and wisdom to go beyond.

INFIRMITY

Do you know someone who seems to always be ill? Is that because they have bad genes or a weak immune system? It could be, but many suffer from infirmity based on spiritual influences or root causes. Some may even accept that this is the burden or the lot that God has for them. This is not to say that the trials that come with disease or sickness cannot be used to strengthen our faith, but God doesn't want us to accept a wrong belief or perspective. Jesus rebuked all of it!

Let's take a look at 3 John and gain the right outlook.

Beloved, I pray that you may prosper in all things and be in health, just as your soul prospers.

— *3 John 1:2*

He wants us to prosper in every way, including our health. Think of how our health impacts everything else in our lives. It's essential to life! God wants us to live free from every form of bondage, even in our bodies.

God desires for us to prosper in all areas. He wants us to

overcome everything that limits us, and He is waiting to help. More than anything, He desires that close relationship of a loving father with us. Overcoming is not achieved through or based upon our human striving; it is achieved through the love of the Father, who gave His only Son for us to experience the fullness of life.

BELIEF VS. CONVICTIONS

Once again, I can't stress enough the importance of taking inventory of our beliefs in this hour. Every belief we have is not a principled conviction of value. Certain convictions aren't worth having. A person's individual convictions should be of great benefit to themselves and others; it should not be self-centered. Abraham Lincoln's conviction led him to emancipate slaves. Martin Luther King's conviction led him to gather hundreds of thousands to Washington, D.C., for the fight for civil rights. David's conviction caused him to take out Goliath! God gives us a conviction and places it within our conscience for us to believe better. When we receive higher insight and believe better, we discover and establish more successful, effective, and productive ways of living. Limitations become a thing of the past, and prosperity becomes the present reality and door to the future.

MEDITATION FOR APPLICATION

Set aside 15-30 minutes each day to commune with God. Each day read and meditate on one of the Scriptures listed below. Follow these steps.

1. Go to a quiet place without distraction.

2. Play a praise song and just listen to the words.

3. Ask God to reveal His heart and meaning to you as you read the Scriptures.

4. Write your reflections below or in your journal.

5. Read the Scriptures daily so you receive maximum revelation.

3 John 1:2 NKJV
Deuteronomy 8:18 NKJV
Colossians 2:8 KJV
John 5:5-6 TPT

MOMENTS OF REFLECTION

1. Think of the man at the Pool of Bethesda. Are you acting like him? Is God telling you to "pick up your pallet and walk," yet you tell Him why you can't?

2. What traditions of mankind limit you? How can you invite Holy Spirit to lead you in His ways to avoid manmade traps?

Notes:

THE RISE OF THE OVERCOMER

CHAPTER 9
ARISE BY FAITH AND MOVE IN VICTORY

For whatever is born of God overcomes the world. And this is the victory that has overcome the world—our faith.

— *1 John 5:4*

I recently sought the Lord, and He began to speak to me and challenge me to believe for something miraculous. He led me to look at the situations, events, and attitudes surrounding Mary and Elizabeth when the angel was sent by God to declare the Lord's plan.

In Luke chapter one, God sent the angel Gabriel to a virgin girl named Mary, who was already pledged to be married. The angel announced to Mary that she was blessed and chosen by the Lord to receive God's holy seed and give birth to the Messiah, the son of the Most High.

Mary's response to the news was, "How will this happen, seeing that I am a virgin?"

The angel responded by saying, "The Holy Spirit will come upon you! It will be established by the power of the Most High."

Many of us, like Elizabeth, feel that our best days have already passed. But God says, "Don't believe the lies. The world, the flesh and the devil will deceive you from seeing and hearing what I desire for you to move into. Lift up your eyes. You are here for a reason. If you will fully believe Me once again, you will conceive a new thing and move into that next portion of covenant that is much greater than the former."

In the days ahead the Lord is preparing us for some things that will not make sense to our natural minds. We won't have the ability to comprehend how these things will unfold, but God's Spirit will overshadow us and empower us for the journey. Like Mary, it will take courage, faith, obedience, and sacrifice to bring forth God's purposes. It will also take a new level of dedication so that God will have the preeminence and all earthly distractions are shut down and dismantled.

But seek first the kingdom of God and His righteousness, and all these things shall be added to you.

— Matthew 6:33

Faith is a now substance. We must conceive what God is releasing now! And we must respond now! Lives are at stake and souls are at risk. We must hear and obey what God is saying NOW! Multitudes and multitudes are waiting for us to believe what God says about us so their lives can change. Listen to the voice of the Lord saying, "With man it is impossible, but not with God. For all things are possible with God."

Raise your expectations and respond quickly to the God of Miracles. He is the one who causes all things to be possible in the midst of difficulty or failure. His power supersedes the impotence of humanity. Let the Most High take you beyond for the glory of His name. You are somebody's miracle.

If you're struggling with trusting God, bypass your mind and just open your mouth. Like Jesus' mother, Mary, we can have a moment of repentance and say, "Nevertheless, I am the Lord's servant. Let it be unto me as You have said." God wants to inconvenience us and disrupt our comfort so that many will know Him in the coming days. Will you let Him?

AN ENEMY HAS DONE THIS

We must recognize that which opposes us and opens the door for evil to enter into our sphere of authority. Evil comes to weaken, ruin, and destroy the core of our existence. It is sown into our hearts to overtake the good, pure, strong, and healthy areas of our being that God has given us to live peaceful, prosperous lives. Evil is sent, planted, and set against humanity. I know this may be a hard pill to swallow, but hear the truth. We have a real enemy in our garden, our "adversary the devil" (1 Peter 5:8). The enemy stirs up trouble to steal and destroy the plantings of God. We are not to allow ourselves to think this is just the way things are. In 1 Peter we see that the enemy comes and plants evil on purpose.

Be sober, be vigilant; because your adversary the devil walks about like a roaring lion, seeking whom he may devour.

— 1 Peter 5:8

Here is another story Jesus told: "The Kingdom of Heaven is like a farmer who planted good seed in his field. But that night as the workers slept, his enemy came and planted weeds among the wheat, then slipped away. When the crop began to grow and produce grain, the weeds also grew.
"The farmer's workers went to him and said, 'Sir, the field where you planted that good seed is full of weeds! Where did they come from?'

127

"'An enemy has done this!' the farmer exclaimed.
"'Should we pull out the weeds?' they asked.
"'No,' he replied, 'you'll uproot the wheat if you do.
Let both grow together until the harvest. Then I will
tell the harvesters to sort out the weeds, tie them
into bundles, and burn them, and to put the wheat
in the barn.'"

— *Matthew 13:24-30 NLT*

Guard your heart above all else,
for it determines the course of your life.

— *Proverbs 4:23 NLT*

Keep vigilant watch over your heart;
that's where life starts.
Don't talk out of both sides of your mouth;
avoid careless banter, white lies, and gossip.
Keep your eyes straight ahead;
ignore all sideshow distractions.
Watch your step,
and the road will stretch out smooth before you.
Look neither right nor left;
leave evil in the dust.

— *Proverbs 4:23-27 MSG*

So, what is evil? Evil is anything working against any part of your identity, salvation, divine purpose, or prosperity. We have a true enemy who is continuously working against our inheritance through Christ. The thief comes to steal, kill, and destory, but Jesus came that we may have life, yes, abundant life (see John 10:10).

WEAPONS OF THE ENEMY

The devil wishes to weaken us. He does this by causing us to have a divided heart that produces double mindedness, continually questioning the will of God as Eve did. In the following paragraphs I've listed some common ways the devil does that.

1. Deception: Deception creates a divided heart that hinders people from moving into the plan of God for their lives. But God empowers people to overcome deception and stand against it. The more we can stand against evil, the more whole we become within our souls, which ultimately establishes undivided hearts within us.

2. Distraction: Distraction creates a divided heart, pain, rejection, offense, and ambitions and desires that do not align with God's desires.

3. Religion: Religion controls movement. It locks down our purpose and prosperity by causing us to remain comfortable with a form of godliness that denies the power. The word *deny* means *to oppose, reject, refuse, or veto.*

However, Jesus said in Luke 10:18-19, "Listen! I saw Satan fall like lightning from Heaven. And I have given you power to trample upon snakes and scorpions and the power of the enemy!" This is the power, position, and access you are given as a son or daughter of God.

Listen to what Paul writes in Galations:

Now we're no longer living like slaves under the law, but we enjoy being God's very own sons and daughters! And because we're his, we can access everything our Father has—for we are heirs because of what God has done!

— Galations 4:7 TPT

I can remember a time when my husband and I would hear sermon after sermon and prophecy after prophecy, and my husband, who was struggling with his faith and very disheartened during that time, would turn to me and say, "Yeah, but they don't mean any of that for us." He would say these things because he'd experienced so much hurt and disappointment in the younger years of his life from trusted leaders and authority figures.

It would deeply agitate me. I would be so angry when he said that because I would think to myself, "I did not sign up for a life where God looked past me. Nor did I decide to get in the line where God's promises would not be fulfilled and my faith would be completely disregarded. I entered into a covenant with the lover of my soul, the Giver of Life. I rejected every form of disappointment and falsehood to move into the fullness and greatness of His love! I chose the greater portion…the better way! I chose to live and not die."

One day the Lord said, *I will be exalted! Choose ye this day whom you will serve. If you continue to serve the little foxes and hold onto those little offenses that you are choosing to magnify, I will give you over to your choice and you will serve those foxes into the future. I am greater and I will be exalted! I will have a people who lift Me up and glorify My name. If you choose Me, I will lead you into the portion called MORE."*

Direct me, Yahweh, throughout my journey so I can experience your plans for my life. Reveal the life-paths that are pleasing to you. Escort me into your truth; take me by the hand and teach me. For you are

*the God of my salvation; I have wrapped my heart
into yours all day long!*

— *Psalm 25:4-5 TPT*

God is more committed to our destiny than we are. He has an amazing plan for our lives, and He is relentless about us walking in the fullness of that plan. I saw something so profound recently that it caused me to run around my house! I was having a deep God-moment, and then God showed me the sky. I literally saw the blue sky transform into rainbow colors. The Lord said, *You have crossed over into the realm of the Yes and Amen! No longer will you say the sky's the limit, because now the skies, or the heavens, are moving on your behalf and working in your favor. Limitations have been removed!*

So, hear me. If you are hearing Father God say, "No," it is because He's guiding you into or keeping you in the realm of the Yes and Amen. He is not rejecting you or holding anything back from you. It's just the opposite. He is securing you on the path for victory so you can experience the beauty and glory of triumph.

*But you belong to God, my dear children. You have
already won a victory over those people, because the
Spirit who lives in you is greater than the spirit who
lives in the world.*

— *1 John 4:4 NLT*

WHAT FAITH LOOKS LIKE

Faith is a victorious power that triumphs over all the world, its conditions, and its circumstances. It has many applications

131

and attributes. Faith is released through hope and expectation for some form of change or breakthrough to occur on behalf of an individual or a situation. Faith for the Christian believer is demonstrated through testings, trials, experiences, ultimately knowing that God will never fail or forsake us. No matter how bleak circumstances appear to be, God is with us. As it states in 1 John 5:4, faith in God is the power we have to overcome the world in every situation.

TAKING UP AUTHORITY BY FAITH

David took his God-given authority, and by faith he moved in a new way and created a new order. King David brought the Ark of the Covenant up to Jerusalem and placed it among the people. He did not keep with the old system of placing the Ark in a temple. Instead, he placed it within a tent among the people and then offered burnt offerings and sacrifices to the Lord, without the priesthood. This established a new order of worship.

When we use our authority, it pleases God, and He increases our jurisdiction. Jehu was the commander of Israel's army whom God anointed to deal with the evil, ruling spirits in the land. The Lord saw that Jehu did not tolerate evil and he was willing to confront and put to death those things that were contrary to God's will. God looks for those He can send to tear down strongholds and establish His altar in the places or territories He sends them.

When we face off the spirit of religion, tradition, and culture to establish God's Kingdom in the lives and hearts of people, we must use our authority. Nehemiah used his authority and influence to build what God was calling him to build. God gave Nehemiah the authority, blueprint, and resources to rebuild the wall and reestablish God's order in the land. We have to be willing to step up and take up our authority to restore God's order into our homes, workplaces, public facilities, and churches. Evil will be displaced when we do this.

SET APART BY FAITH

Walking by faith requires a level of uncommon obedience that sets us apart from regular human activities and earthly habits, according to the instructions of the Lord. Jesus called the twelve disciples, asking them to leave everything behind. Abraham left a lavish and cushy life in Ur to follow God's calling. He literally packed up everyone and everything and set out on a journey, not fully knowing where he would end up. However, he was willing to go the way of the Lord. His descendants were also called to commit their way to the Lord. Their lives were distinctly marked by the covenant of God, but their faith to obey set them apart from all the other peoples and nations.

We may all have wilderness experiences, where we must depend on the Spirt to lead us. Jesus was led to the wilderness so He could see the overwhelming power of God. Jesus' first lesson to us is that we can overcome the devil, even in our wilderness season.

Jesus was baptized and God thundered from heaven, "This is my beloved Son, in whom I am well pleased" (Matthew 17:5 KJV). This was the announcement of Jesus' position and status to the entire world from the heavenly Father. Certainly, Jesus felt excited about this affirmation. Imagine if God split the skies and said this about you. You would be on top of the world!

Everything Jesus did was a demonstration for us to follow. In Jesus' wilderness experience we see Him facing off the devil, so we'd know how to overcome the devil. Jesus did not start by showing us signs, wonders, and miracles. Instead, He began by demonstrating how to confront the devil, which points to its importance. Strongholds of darkness, generational curses, iniquitous cycles, and evil roots are likely to reproduce when we do not deal with the evil powers working against us.

When we take authority and face off the devil we must say,

133

"I break your power."

By faith he dwelt in the land of promise as in a foreign country, dwelling in tents with Isaac and Jacob, the heirs with him of the same promise.

— Hebrews 11:9

FAITH IN UNCERTAINTY

Some years ago, on a small vintage television in Tallulah, Louisiana, we watched Hurricane Katrina enter the Gulf of Mexico. And hours after, we watched Katrina sweep away our homes, schools, and jobs as the levees in New Orleans began to break. It was very difficult to see our entire livelihood being wiped out, as tons of muddy water continued to pour into the city. I vividly remember going into the kitchen of the old house where we had gone for refuge. I peered through the window at the dark skies and, with tears rolling down my face, I asked the Lord, "Why is this happening? What are you doing?"

He said, "I'm answering your prayers."

I thought long and hard about the prayers I had previously prayed. I couldn't believe I would have ever asked for the devastation that I was witnessing. During the time of evacuation, I sought the Lord in a new way. Life had completely changed, which caused me to do everything differently. I later realized that the prayers the Lord said He was answering were not prayers for destruction but prayers for drastic change that would cause our purpose and path of destiny to be revealed.

At that time, we took our three children and moved into a two-bedroom trailer that was located on a farm in a town that I had never heard of in my entire life. Civilization, to say the least, seemed very far away. As I sought God for help, He began to speak to me clearly. I developed a new level of intimacy with Him. He met with me daily in those fields. My family and I never lacked a thing while we were there.

Was it easy? Heck, no! Every day was a new day of adjustment. Only the grace of God brought us through it. We stayed in that little town for four months. Then we packed up and went back to New Orleans to deal with the ruins.

As we returned, the Lord began to show me a significant parallel between the demolition and rebuilding process of our home and what He was doing in our lives. He revealed to us that the life we had previously been living was just like building a home on a bad or wrong foundation. Before this revelation, we didn't realize that we had begun to subtly conform and live by the words of men instead of listening to and heeding the voice of God. In short, we had been living a lie.

I would like to say it got easier after that, but it did not. The Lord led us through the Valley of the Shadow of Death, where people and things that I dearly loved died and vanished unexpectedly. He allowed certain things to happen to me and my family that are, even now, still indescribable—but He was with us the whole way. That's what mattered. He would not allow anything to overtake us. He spoke words of truth, which strengthened and comforted us, as the enemy continued to cause havoc and wage war against us. But God did not fail us even once!

The Lord strengthened me daily. In the midst of chaos and turmoil, He taught us the reality of spiritual warfare and His overcoming power. He fortified my family and delivered us from massive weapons of evil, and He still does. He brought forth justice and triumph, and we rejoiced. God prevailed!

135

FAITH WORKS BY LOVE

*For when we place our faith in Christ Jesus, there is no
benefit in being circumcised or being uncircumcised.
What is important is faith expressing itself in love.*

— *Galatians 5:6 NLT*

Faith works by love, and perfect love casts out all fear. Our
level of intimate relationship will determine our level of faith.
When we commit ourselves to walk with God, we walk with a
confident expectation, knowing that we're highly favored by the
Lord God Almighty who has established His covenant with us
and is taking us to an enlarged place.

Love and war go together; we will never effectively war for
that which we have no love for. If we truly love something, we
will fight for it. We cannot love something we are not willing to
war for. Jesus loved us enough to face off the devil and defeat
Him.

Our faith action must be based on a strong relationship with
God. We must trust that He will never leave nor forsake us. He
will always be there and give us what we need to stand in faith
and do the works we're called to do.

Years ago I would listen to "faith preachers," who claimed
that we can move mountains if we just have faith. They would
say, "You have such little faith, and that has placed you in the
place you are in." I felt condemned in my relationship with God.
Crying in the car, crying out to God, I told Him everything I was
doing to build faith.

Then I asked Him, "How do I get faith?"

He answered, *Robyn, do you believe I love you? Do you
believe I love enough to die for you? If you believe in My love*

for you, then you have faith in Me. You do not have small faith. Stop believing that. I will do everything I can to support you and establish faith.

God was building faith for faith! I had no clue at that time that "faith works by love" is a Scripture in the Bible (see Galatians 5:6). God demonstrated it to me through that conversation. *If you believe I love you that much, My daughter, you have faith.*

When I arrived at Glory of Zion many years later, one Sunday Dr. Chuck Pierce said, "Faith works by love. That's what the Bible says." That is when I realized the principle God had taught me was a Scripture! Intimacy with the Lord builds faith. To war against the evil one, we have to submit to God, grow in relationship, and then take action.

Therefore submit to God. Resist the devil and he will flee from you.

— *James 4:7*

I had to trust God and receive that His plan for me included marriage. Initially I didn't want to be married because I didn't trust people with my heart. However, God's plan was greater than my own plan. God kept placing James on my path. No matter how I felt about it, He continued to stick to His plan. I continued to run into James because God was placing us together.

This freaked me out! I had never seen marriage as a part of my life. I thought it was for weak women, because of wrong examples I had witnessed growing up. Men seemed to cause women to be weak, and I feared being weak. I even tried to set James up with other women.

But when the Lord told me He was putting me together with my husband, He said He would put love in my heart for James. I had to submit to a plan different than my own. I had to get past

137

my own mind. I shudder to think what would have happened if I had not submitted to God's plan. God faithfully brought us together in marriage and He has kept us all these years. He put James in my life so both James and I could fulfill what we were called and destined to do as one.

FAITH LEADS TO ACTION

I decided to follow God and not resist a relationship with James, which is an example of my faith ultimately leading to the right action. Jesus told Peter to prove his love for the Lord by taking the action of feeding His sheep.

> *He said to him the third time, "Simon, son of Jonah, do you love Me?" Peter was grieved because He said to him the third time, "Do you love Me?" And he said to Him, "Lord, You know all things; You know that I love You." Jesus said to him, "Feed My sheep."*

> — *John 21:17*

This is an example of faith that works by love. The Lord was saying to Peter, "If you love Me, this is what you will do. "

Love is a faith action that is tied to a strong hope or belief. It creates a deep conviction that inspires us to do all that God asks of us. We have true success in our faith by obeying every word that comes out of God's mouth. We can trust the love of our heavenly Father. Even when situations are uncomfortable, we can walk in the confidence of our covenant knowing He will order our steps and fulfill His will. No matter what we face, we will reap the benefits of having God on our side.

A PRAYING MOM'S FAITH ACTION

A dear friend in Christ shared this story of how his mom's faith action opened the door for a change in his life. His life was totally transformed because of her act of faith.

In April of 2005 my mom and I attended an annual prophetic watchmen conference in Florida hosted by a leader in the prophetic movement. A prominent prophet was the last speaker for the conference, which ended Saturday afternoon three hours before I had a flight I needed to catch.

My mom and her best friend had driven to Florida for the conference so they could drive me to the Pensacola airport. When it was time for us to leave, my mom looked at me with this deep, perplexed look, like she was about to do something crazy.

I said, "No, Ma. Don't do it."

She said, "The prophet who spoke at the end of the conference is supposed to take you to the airport."

I said, "No, absolutely not! He doesn't know us like that! Don't embarrass me, woman!"

She took my wrist and dragged me to the front to speak to the gentleman. He obviously had a line of people waiting to speak to him, but we waited patiently. I waited behind her like a shamed puppy.

When it was our turn to talk to him, she boldly stated, "My son needs a ride to the airport. May he ride with you, if it's no trouble?"

The man didn't hesitate and said, "Yes. Go follow

139

my assistant, and stay with him until we are ready to leave."

Riding with this prophet to the airport gave me an opportunity to get to know him and tell my story. A few months after that, I was in a financial mess way over my head. Once again, my mom boldly called the man and told him to contact me so he could help.

Mom always made sure I had a father in my life. I tried to do things on my own, but I needed someone to guide me.

The first thing the man said when I entered his office for the first time was, "You need a father in the spirit, and you need a father in the world."

My natural dad was always there but he only could take me so far. This prophet became the father I needed to fulfill my destiny.

If my friend's mother had not taken a faith-filled action, his life would not have been aligned with God's plan for him. Faith actions are bold steps that God directs us to take to see His power and goodness at work in our lives.

LIVING THE ABUNDANT LIFE

I was recently studying the concept of abundant life that is mentioned in John 10:10. The Scripture says,

> *The thief does not come except to steal, and to kill, and to destroy. I have come that they may have life, and that they may have* it *more abundantly.*

> — *John 10:10*

The Greek word for *have*, when it pertains to having life

abundantly, means to *hold, keep, or possess. Abundant Life* means: *to the full, in the sense of beyond, super abundant in quantity, superior in quality, excessive by implication, exuberant, exceedingly, abundantly, above more, and highly beyond measure.*

The Greek root word, which in the Word is *abundant,* stems from and means *all around, on every side.* This is what God wants for all of us. God was speaking of a desire far beyond what each of us can even imagine for ourselves! He's declaring, "I have come that you may possess, hold, and keep an exuberant measure of super-abundant life!"

This is beyond our comprehension or human level of understanding. God just wants us to believe Him for it, to allow ourselves to be wrapped up in it, submitted to this new truth and way and direction. God wants much more for us; where we are now is not it.

When I was ministering in Lafayette, Louisiana, I met someone who was doubting God's call on her life. I asked her, "What if you are the next Esther? Can you believe God for what you need in order to become the next reformer of your generation?"

She looked at me with cautious faith and said, "Yes."

He is the God of the impossible. He creates and furnishes our lives with limitless possibilities, even when it seems impossible to the human mind. Our expectations of God should never be limited to what we can think or imagine Him doing. We should expectantly call upon Him to display the wonders of His power that are beyond our comprehension.

Do not say, "I will recompense evil";
Wait for the LORD, and He will save you.

— Proverbs 20:22

There are times we all try to figure out how God is going to do something. However, we must be so submitted that we don't question the how. We must trust Him and expect Him to deliver what He promises. Those who trust in the Lord will be like Mount Zion; they will not be moved. Following His wisdom and commands empowers us to stand in faith and authority.

Using our authority is also a faith act. When Jehu was anointed by Elisha's young prophet, he declared to him that he was now to be king over all of Israel and had been chosen to bring destruction upon the house of Ahab and Queen Jezebel. Immediately, he went out against them and executed judgment just as he had been anointed and charged to do. He had to rid the land of their evil practices because it was operating within his boundaries.

In every place the Lord calls us, He requires us to set boundary lines. For example, we should be able to say, "This is where I work or dwell, or this is what I oversee and care for." This identification gives definition to our boundaries. Abraham had to set boundaries. David had to set boundaries. Jehu had to set boundaries. This is what caused them to take dominion and fulfill the purposes of God.

Often, we are not standing where God has positioned us to stand because we have not exercised the authority that we've been given to successfully establish peace, productivity, and prosperity within our boundaries. We must mark our territory to make others, especially opposers, know that it is under our jurisdiction. Our supervision or oversight will be unsuccessful if we do not use our authority. That's why so many in the body of Christ have been weakened and plundered. They have not drawn the boundary lines. They have not said, "This is what belongs to me!"

Setting boundaries causes us to establish, protect, and keep the order of that which has been delegated to us. Any evil that crosses that line will be met with a rude awakening. We must realize that Satan is constantly trespassing in our home, our workplace, and the lives of our children. We must rise in authority and set a stopping point, lifting our voices and saying to him, "You have no place here!"

Forty-two-year-old Rosa Parks knew how to stand in her authority as a colored woman in 1955. When she was asked to give up her "colored section" seat on the bus, she recognized that someone was crossing the line and she refused to do so. Although she was arrested, tried, and found guilty of violating segregation laws, this incident initiated a major thrust that caused the Supreme Court to rule one year later that bus segregation is unconstitutional. This is what it means to draw the line, mark our boundaries, and stand in our place.

Remember what the Lord said to Joshua when He first commissioned him:

> *Moses My servant is dead. Now therefore, arise, go over this Jordan, you and all this people, to the land which I am giving to them—the children of Israel. Every place that the sole of your foot will tread upon I have given you, as I said to Moses. From the wilderness and this Lebanon as far as the great river, the River Euphrates, all the land of the Hittites, and to the Great Sea toward the going down of the sun, shall be your territory. No man shall be able to stand before you all the days of your life; as I was with Moses, so I will be with you. I will not leave you nor forsake you.*
>
> *— Joshua 1:2-5*

God says the same to us in this hour. The land is yours. Wherever you place your feet, it is yours.

We must set clear boundary lines so we can evict the enemy. If we don't set boundary lines, how can we legitimately remove the adversary that trespasses? If we haven't set boundary lines, he doesn't even know he is trespassing. We have given him full access!

As I said before, the devil is invading every space he can. If it's your sphere of influence, then you are the only one who can evict him. Draw the line and kick him out. Take back what belongs to you! Selah.

MEDITATION FOR APPLICATION

Set aside 15-30 minutes each day to commune with God. Each day read and meditate on one of the Scriptures listed below. Follow these steps.

1. Go to a quiet place without distraction.

2. Play a praise song and just listen to the words.

3. Ask God to reveal His heart and meaning to you as you read the Scriptures.

4. Write your reflections below or in your journal.

5. Read the Scriptures daily so you receive maximum revelation.

1 John 5:4 NKJV
Galatians 5:6 NLT
1 John 4:16-19 NKJV

MOMENTS OF REFLECTION

1. Are you in a place of uncertainty right now? Focus on believing He has the best for you and speak it out loud in your prayer time.

2. Where is the devil infiltrating your life? What boundary lines do you need to set to keep the devil at bay?

3. Think of the bold faith action of the mom in the story. What bold faith action do you need to take?

Notes:

CHAPTER 10
RECIEVE POWER AND BE MADE NEW

When I was a teenager, my mom remarried. It felt like I no longer had a place in life because the new husband wanted to have a new family. At the same time, my father was on the other side of town, living with a woman he had fallen in love with and her children. I felt very abandoned and alone for most of my high school years. I no longer knew where I belonged.

Knowing what I know now, I realize this was the entry point for many depraved behaviors and attitudes that settled in my heart and rerouted my life. Of course, I began to act out of character and get entangled with people that were lewd, deviant, and morally bankrupt. But at least they were present—that's what I felt. Their unprincipled presence gave me an escape from the feelings of orphancy from the lack of my parents' presence during that time.

It wasn't until many years later that I was able to look back and see that I had been suffering from heartache, which had led me to feel like an orphan. The rejection and pain I had felt made me feel something that wasn't actually true; my feelings had created a huge distortion. Although I had felt neglected and pushed to the side because my parents seemed to be preoccupied, the truth is I had never been parentless. I had just needed someone to speak and empower me to know the difference, so I could manage my emotions and learn to respond properly.

This is how life looks for many of us. Whenever our sense of normalcy, safety, and peace is disrupted, we react out of fear. Or when a different factor or new dynamic unexpectedly shows up, we can feel a substantial amount of stress, which results in a flood of emotional anxiety and racing thoughts. Before we know it, we can quickly get caught in a tailspin that produces much more chaos and confusion than the initial situation that started the trouble.

We see this pattern with many of the Hollywood celebrities we love and admire. When they first start their careers, they seem to be on top of the world! They are adored by millions of fans. They make incredible amounts of money. They get to do what they love to do and travel all around the world. Then all of a sudden, things change! We hear the daunting news reports about some form of trouble they have gotten themselves into because they no longer have ties with their families or their support systems. We hear about drug addictions, promiscuous lifestyles, or other bad decisions.

These perturbing things begin to take place when there is a great need for some form of guidance to support the superstar through the painstaking process of becoming famous and responsibly stewarding that level of fame. Through trials of life, we discover that we have real needs that are essential to living a successful life. One of those essentials is aligning with the right people. This is key to dispelling the toxic emotions that lead to poor choices. Having the right conversation with the right person can give the correct perspective for finding a viable solution and possibility. This is just one way to overcome.

Rather than allowing negative feelings to rewrite our story or disqualify us from our path of destiny, we can use our reservoir of internal strength to manage our thoughts and balance our emotions. When change is managed, we grow and flourish, transforming into new beings. Turmoil becomes the fertilizer for our transformation.

BECOME GOD'S GIFT TO THE WORLD

A few years ago, when my family and I traveled to Israel for a vacation, I had the privilege of meeting a very wise man. He initiated an interesting conversation that sparked my interest. He said, "Do you want to know the secret to our success as God's beloved people? Many don't understand why we are so prosperous and wealthy. We are prosperous because of God. God in all of His wisdom placed a gift on the inside of us. It can never be stolen or destroyed because it is on the inside of us. So it doesn't matter what our enemies do to us, wherever we go we will still prosper because we always use our gifts. Even if we are driven away from our land, wherever we go the land prospers because we use what God put in us."

> *A man's gift makes room for him,*
> *And brings him before great men.*
>
> — *Proverbs 18:16*

This leads me to a very foundational and significant truth: Know that you're the gift. Don't waste time and get hung up trying to discover and define your gifts, talents, or skill sets. Nothing is wrong with honing your skills and talents. That's actually beneficial and commendable, but this is different. Know that you are the gift that God chose to bless the earth. You are the brand that others are waiting on. It's what innately flows out of you when you're not even thinking about it. It's the unique creative flow, bold expressions, and strong convictions that you wake up with every day. It's who you are!

Be who you are organically. No matter what happens in life,

don't allow anything to stop you from being your authentic self and using what God has placed inside of you. Your perspective, personality, and purpose plays a huge part in the prosperity of your bloodline, community or spheres of influence. Everything you are is capable of carrying restoration and redemption. Let God use you to bless the world!

His sons and daughter are charged and trusted with the responsibility of bringing light to the dark places of earth. We must unapologetically begin to be who God has created us to be so the love and life that we carry begin to heal the hopeless and the hurting. Mountains move, waters part, and lives are forever changed when we give ourselves permission to be the one that God can use.

DON'T SETTLE, JUST SETTLE IT

Don't settle! This is a very common phrase that I hear today in conversations amongst various groups and individuals, secular and non-secular. Although I must admit it surprises me more when I hear it within Christian settings. Why am I surprised? Well, I'm glad you asked. Let me tell you why.

I believe well-meaning, good-hearted, genuinely concerned people want nothing but the best for us. With that being said, we must look at their reason for telling others "Don't settle!" When I look throughout the Bible, this is not a topic that I see commonly addressed. "Why are you settling?" is not a statement that I regularly come across when reading God's Word. So why do we speak of "settling" as if it's one of the things God hates most?

Jesus did not have to convince his disciples to not settle. No one had to convince Paul, Peter, James, or John to not settle. Even in the Old Testament, when the Lord spoke to the Israelites and told them not to intermarry with women from other nations,

He did not speak of settling. He told His people not to mingle with the foreigners because they would turn their hearts away from the Lord to follow after other gods. It was not to imply that somehow they were settling for less.

That's what the concept of "settling" does. It implies that one thing is greater than the other, or one person is somehow of more value than another. This is not God's perspective. The reason we don't see this type of language being used or this concept being fostered in the Bible is simply because it is an erroneous way of seeing people or situations. It causes us to make wrong judgments.

God sees good and evil, life and death, and light and darkness. He sees the light of truth and the mask of deception, and He sees how each of these influences the hearts of His people. As the Creator and progenitor of all, He does not view the world by the standards of men. He peers at it through His own lenses and judges all by His righteous order and design.

As I've previously stated, His ways are not our ways. His standards will produce everything He has promised. So what's His order? What's His answer to the cultural issue of "settling"? How do we overcome and know that we are not settling or processing life from a faulty perspective?

Let's look at Abraham. Romans 4:16-17 refers to Abraham as the example and father of faith. So if we want to receive the best outcome for any decision we make or action we take, we should look to the father of faith. He received every promise God made and considered Him faithful.

> *Against all odds, when it looked hopeless, Abraham believed the promise and expected God to fulfill it. He took God at his word, and as a result he became the father of many nations. God's declaration over him came to pass: "Your descendants will be so*

many that they will be impossible to count!"

— *Romans 4:18 TPT*

Let's look again at what we just read. Abraham believed God's promise and He confidently expected Him to fulfill it. Without doubt or hesitation, He took God at His word. And as a result, he became exactly what God promised, the father of many nations. Wow!

The only thing Abraham had to do was follow the instructions and he would receive the fulfillment of every promise God made. He believed God enough to respond in faith with faithful obedience.

If you will only obey me,
you will have plenty to eat.

— *Isaiah 1:19 NLT*

The principle we learn here is that when we obey the Lord, we receive His best for our lives. We never have to worry about settling for anything less when we believe His word and obey His directives. His words of instruction give us the roadmap to the abundant life He promised. In Deuteronomy 28, The Word of God depicts a deluge of blessing for those who are obedient. God promises to bless the individual, the fruit of their womb, their barns, baskets, livestock, storehouses, and land. He promises to destroy their enemies and to always position them as the head and not the tail. He declares to the heavens and the earth that those who carefully obey will forever be at the top and never at the bottom. His words are sent out to establish it. God never settles when He bestows blessings on His children. He is more than generous!

Also, let's be sure not to forget one of the key factors of Abraham's success: Abraham expected God to fulfill His word! We must let His promises settle in our hearts and become the fuel that drives us to obey, even when we don't want to. If we practice trusting the Father and taking Him at His word, we can confidently expect Him to do exactly what He said. This is how we settle the matter and overcome the fear or temptation that comes with the concept of settling. Stay expectant and the Lord will bring the manifestation.

SERVE THE GREATER ONE IN YOU

Recently I was sitting at my kitchen table, having my morning coffee. This is the time I quiet myself to have a peaceful time of fellowship with Father. During this time He spoke something so profound to me that it made me question and consider my true inner beliefs. He asked, *Robyn, do you trust Me?*

I quickly responded, "Of course I trust you! You can do anything."

Then He asked me another question. *Do you trust Me to be just as powerful within you?*

In that moment, I had to honestly assess my heart and look at the truth. My answer was "no." He knew the answer before He asked the question.

Why was this the case though? I knew most of the Scriptures that clearly depict and state all that God can do through weak, earthen vessels like me. I quickly recalled 1 John 4:4, Ephesians 3:20, Luke 10:19, and 2 Corinthians 4:7. So why was I struggling in this area?

We now have this light shining in our hearts, but we ourselves are like fragile clay jars containing this great treasure. This makes it clear that our great power is from God, not from ourselves.

— *2 Corinthians 4:7 NLT*

The truth is that I was focusing on my own strength, not God's. I was considering my limited capacity and not God's limitless power and abilities. God showed me how dangerous this can be when there's so much at stake. We need His supernatural power and authority to complete every assignment the Lord calls us to. Our strength and power cannot fulfill the supernatural call of God!

In today's world, when society is deeply misguided and filled with distortion, we cannot afford to look at ourselves in a fleshly manner. This is something we must overcome! From moment to moment, we must practice reminding ourselves that God is abiding on the inside of us for His covenant plan to be established. He is dwelling within us for the sole purpose of accomplishing His work through us. When we are confidently walking with the Lord and seeking His kingdom above all things, we can walk in His righteousness and boldly do what He's called us to do, without any hesitation.

We must serve His purposes in spirit and in truth. As stated before in a previous chapter, when we agree with the truth of God, we are able to release His power and presence into any situation. We can't believe what others are saying about us or what we say about ourselves and be powerful at the same time. Much of that chatter is demonically motivated. We must not give room to anything that keeps us from living in the power of God's truth, which is already at work within us.

We must not give ear to anything that keeps us from believing in the power of 1 John 4:4, which says (NLT):

*But you belong to God, my dear children. You have
already won a victory over those people, because
the Spirit who lives in you is greater than the spirit
who lives in the world.*

When we are abiding in Christ, He is abiding in us. Who we are with the Lord is vastly different than who we are without Him. Let your roots go down deep into this truth. In Him, we are brilliant, powerful, and fully capable of doing anything we are called to do. If we ever allow ourselves to believe that we are inadequate, incompetent, or incapable, we will be given to lies that weaken our spiritual identity and cause us to proceed with a very distorted view. Truth will always empower us, and lies will continue to weaken us. Make a decision to believe God and become the person you were predestined to be before the earth ever knew your name. This is my prayer for you:

I pray that you will never stop overcoming and deflating the schemes of the devil. As you rise and step into a new life, may your words be effectual, may your deeds be fruitful, may your strength be supernatural, and may your rewards be plentiful. In Yeshua's name. Amen.

MEDITATION FOR APPLICATION

Set aside 15-30 minutes each day to commune with God. Each day read and meditate on one of the Scriptures listed below. Follow these steps.

1. Go to a quiet place without distraction.

2. Play a praise song and just listen to the words.

3. Ask God to reveal His heart and meaning to you as you read the Scriptures.

4. Write your reflections below or in your journal.

5. Read the Scriptures daily so you receive maximum revelation.

Proverbs 18:16 NKJV
Romans 4:18 TPT
Isaiah 1:19 NLT
Deuteronomy 28 NKJV
2 Corinthians 4:7 NLT
1 John 4:4 NLT

Moments of Reflection

1. Do you have gifts that lie dormant? What are the gifts you can use to bring a light into the world and prosper?

2. What has stopped you from being your authentic self? Take a moment to recognize the things that have stolen areas of your identity.

3. What's the real reason you settle for less in life? How do you overcome a mindset or practice of settling?

4. Meditate on the prayer at the end of Chapter 10 for seven days or longer.

Notes:

THE RISE OF THE OVERCOMER

CHAPTER 11
GOD OVERCAME, NOW WE OVERCOME

Your loving heavenly Father loves you more than you can ever imagine, and He wants you to overcome. He gave His Son so that you would have a joyful, triumphant life, no matter what happens in this world. Jesus's blood secured your portion of God's ever-flowing abundant life. Your troubles will never outlast God because He has already overcome.

> *These things I have spoken to you, that in Me you may have peace. In the world you will have tribulation; but be of good cheer, I have overcome the world.*

> — *John 16:33*

When God created Adam in the Garden, he took him from the dust of the ground, breathed His breath into man's nostrils, and formed the first living person. He was taken from the soil of the earth, and this became a part of him for the generations to come. This reveals the connection man has to the world and all of its pleasures, structures, ideologies, and cultural behaviors.

From the time we are born and throughout adulthood, we are given over to the dictates of the world through traditions, systems, and culture. Our flesh is connected to all of it in one way or another. This means that our appetites, ambitions, and actions are all tied to the natural form of being, not our spiritual being. Operating out of our spiritual identity seems very foreign for most of us.

Out of habit and cultural pressures, we usually focus our efforts on trying to survive or thrive within a world order that we were created to overcome and govern by the grace given to us by God. A person who is authorized to implement order and oversight over a sphere of influence should never allow others to take their position or stand in their stead and speak on their behalf. Another authority will naturally bring in another order, completely undermining and negating what has already been established. This can cause a stirring of confusion and division, so we must be very careful not to allow any other variables to interfere with, diminish, or corrupt that which we're called to govern through our identity in Christ.

This is what happened in the Garden when Adam and Eve allowed the serpent to have a voice of authority. When the serpent spoke a different truth to the man and woman, he questioned the sincerity and validity of God's word and promise to Adam and Eve. This was huge. As a result, Adam and Eve began to doubt the intentions of their Creator. They no longer saw Him as their Father; they saw Him as a deceiver, as someone who was swindling them and trying to deceive them. The person who was supposed to be their protector, provider, confidant, and greatest supporter was now perceived as their opponent.

The enemy does the same thing today. The false truth that their adversary was able to speak to them altered and invalidated their entire existence. How, you ask? Because they were only created for the purposes the Lord had spoken to them.

We must understand why the enemy does this. He plants deception in our hearts so that we won't be who God has created us to be. If we become who God created us to be, then we will accomplish the things God created us to accomplish. This ultimately destroys all the works of the devil and evicts darkness.

Here's the warning: We must guard our heart and use our authority before the enemy usurps it. We open our mouth and shut down anything that brings in the wrong influence into the atmosphere. Our voice is power! When we use it, we drive out every opposition and we establish or maintain peace.

Anytime others can speak into our lives and cause us to take our eyes off God and turn us away from the truth that He has spoken, we will forfeit our purpose and identity. Deception causes derailment. Period. We can't experience the fulfillment of God's promises by living outside of His Word. His Word is what holds the power of our human existence, and His presence is what we need to live a life of wholeness and peace.

> *Little children, you are from God and have overcome them, for he who is in you is greater than he who is in the world.*

> *— 1 John 4:4 ESV*

A popular movie called *The Lord of the Rings* depicts the real-life struggle between man and the desire for power and self-gratification. In the film, a young man learns that a ring has the power to control all of humanity and affect the entire world through evil temptations. This power is especially formidable over the person who possesses the ring. Through a series of the most damnable, tumultuous events and the loving faithfulness of reliable friends, he overcomes the temptations and hardships that besiege him. He finally destroys the ring and all its power by casting it into the lake of fire where it was formed.

These temptations manifest within the flesh and imaginations of mankind. They are linked to impulsive desires that are formed outside of true love. These desires tend to give humans a sense of happiness, freedom, or, sometimes, even fulfillment. But the gratification quickly fades, leaving people with a need for something more. So here lies the unadulterated truth:

161

The love of God is and always will be the only source of true fulfillment for the souls of men and women.

When these fleshly impulses are subdued and overcome, we can live a life of fruitfulness and prosperity that is pleasing in every way. God gives us life, liberty, peace, and provision so that we can overcome anything that hinders us. However, the most powerful gift that He's given us is His Spirit. This means that everything we face in this life must submit to the greatness of God that is on the inside of us. Demons must flee. Mountains must move. And the earth must bow. This is the power that He has freely given to His sons and daughters!

CONFIDENCE IN GOD'S LOVE OVERCOMES

We have to come to know and believe the love that God has for us. We must believe this in every part of our being so we can stand firm in evil times. God is love. If we abide in love, we abide in Him and we are continuously covered by Him. This is our confidence.

> *And so we know and rely on the love God has for us. God is love. Whoever lives in love lives in God, and God in them. This is how love is made complete among us so that we will have confidence on the day of judgment: In this world we are like Jesus. There is no fear in love. But perfect love drives out fear, because fear has to do with punishment. The one who fears is not made perfect in love. We love because he first loved us.*

> — *1 John 4:16-19 NIV*

1 John 4:16 states that we must understand and be fully reliant upon the love that God has for us. That means we must have great, intimate knowledge of God's love and be firmly convinced that this love belongs to each of us and perfects every area of our lives. Lay hold of this revelation! It is given specifically for you.

Many of us begin to squirm and wrestle with this truth. In our western culture we're taught that we must learn and achieve more to be more. So subconsciously we feel like we should strive to know more so that we can be more. Then one day, after we have met all the requirements, we'll have the ability to be able to attain and do more, perpetuating the systemic cycle of continuous striving. That wrong belief is completely contrary to the Word of God.

We spend most of our lives trying to attain a certain number of degrees or a certain level of experience or get to a certain status so that we can gain a space of acceptance, but that is not what we're created for. We are created for love and fruitfulness. We are created to fill the earth with the fragrance of our God and to display the beauty of knowing Him.

When we don't know the love of God, we strive for the love of men. The voids in our souls will always keep us yearning for love, acceptance, and affirmation because at the foundational level we are tormented by the fear of not experiencing what we yearn for. As a result, we run from person to person, city to city, or organization to organization, constantly looking for something to give us a sense of love. We begin to chase after what the world and the flesh have convinced us will satisfy our longing for greatness or fulfillment. The longing continues within and is never satisfied. Why? Because external trappings can't satisfy internal conditions.

Instead of pursuing the world's way, we are to plunge into the sea of God's love and go deep. We shut off everything else and fix our attention completely on him. We stop our routine livinggand unfulfillingghabitssbecause there is so much more life in God. He hasslimitless doorss open for us and favor beyond comprehension because He longs to make His love real in our lives. Don't hesitate or remain apprehensive. You will be forever changed and eternally grateful. Just stop everything and make room for God.

Understand this: God is a spirit. When we begin to seek Him through Bible reading, prayer, or worship, it connects us to His Spirit. This is how He satisfies the spirit of a man, through fellowship and communion.

Everything that God expresses is a different facet of purposeful love. He is wisdom, patience, clarity, instruction, and a very faithful guide who keeps us from stumbling. He is strength for the weary, faith for the weak, hope for the hopeless, and grace for the wicked. He is love in its purest and most potent form.

We are called to continually express those different facets and attributes of our heavenly Father. When we know who we are as sons and daughters, we manifest the essence of our beloved Creator. We move in His great power, might, and authority, along with love, compassion, and generosity.

Being confidently rooted in this eternal, unconditional love is the key that we need to unlock the destiny of human souls and nations. This key is to always be carried within our hearts to obtain victory in every season and situation for salvation no matter where we go, what we face, or who we're sent to. This is how we overcome!

GOD'S PROMISES TO THE OVERCOMER

The Scriptures below give insight for us to confidently know the hope of our calling and the rewards of remaining faithful amid testings and trying times. Be of good cheer and take courage! Remember, He has overcome and so will you! The Greatest and Highest of All lives on the inside of you, and you dwell within Him. Nothing in this life will ever have the potential, capacity, or capability of separating you from the One who has defeated the devil and is seated forever in victory.

He who has an ear, let him hear what the Spirit says to the churches. To him who overcomes I will give to eat from the tree of life, which is in the midst of the Paradise of God.

— Revelation 2:7

He who has an ear, let him hear what the Spirit says to the churches. He who overcomes shall not be hurt by the second death.

— Revelation 2:11

To him who overcomes I will give some of the hidden manna to eat. And I will give him a white stone, and on the stone a new name written which no one knows except him who receives it.

— Revelation 2:17

*And he who overcomes, and keeps My works until
the end, to him I will give power over the nations–
"He shall rule them with a rod of iron;
They shall be dashed to pieces like the potter's
vessels"–
as I also have received from My Father; and I will
give him the morning star.*

— *Revelation 2:26-28*

*He who overcomes [the world through believing that Jesus
is the son of God]]will accordingly be dressed
in white clothing and will never blot out his name
from the Book of Life,and I will confess and openly
acknowledge his name before My Father and before
His angels [saying that he is one of Mine].*

— *Revelation 3:5 AMP*

*He who overcomes, I will make him a pillar in the
temple of My God, and he shall go out no more. I
will write on him the name of My God and the name
of the city of My God, the New Jerusalem, which
comes down out of heaven from My God. And* I will
write on him *My new name.*

— *Revelation 3:12*

*To him who overcomes I will grant to sit with Me on
My throne, as I also overcame and sat down with My
Father on His throne.*

— *Revelation 3:21*

166

But hold your hope firmly to the end and you will experience life and deliverance.

— Matthew 24:13 TPT

PROPHETIC WORD TO THE OVERCOMER

———◆━◆━◆━◆━———

The Lord says, *This double portion that you are now receiving is not just for you–it is sent into all the earth! The greater portion is for the greater works that I Am sending you to do in this hour. As I release everything that I Am into you, begin to move into all the earth—from corner to corner, from coast to coast, from sea to shining sea—because I Am doing a new thing, and I Am doing it through My body. As I release the bread of life once again, receive every bit of it, receive a full measure, receive a full portion; I Am going to change the earth through the portion that I Am giving to you this hour!*

Prophetic Word by Robyn Vincent
Glory of Zion International
November 2022

ABOUT THE AUTHOR

Robyn Vincent is an ordained minister and prophet at Glory of Zion International and Global Spheres Inc., and she speaks very passionately from the heart of God. She and her husband, James Vincent, travel and minister around the globe, bringing transformational power and insight to individuals, communities, and regions. Their infectious boldness and passion awaken hearts throughout the earth.

For more than two decades, Robyn has diligently and faithfully served, trained, and taught to equip people around the globe. She is an inspiring speaker, teacher, author, and mentor, as well as a relationship consultant and certified life coach. Robyn is widely recognized for weaving her strong prophetic gifting with transparent dialogue to empower lives with immense freedom and transformation. She fervently delivers messages of redemption, restoration, and recovery to see lasting change and reformation established for all.

She enjoys listening to different styles of music and reading authentic life stories and biographies. She also enjoys watching and attending sports events. Most of all, she loves spending quality time with family and close friends.

Robyn and James reside in Texas. They have five beautiful children and a grandchild. They serve faithfully at the Global Spheres Center under the leadership of Dr. Chuck Pierce.

THE RISE OF THE OVERCOMER

References

Strong, James. *The New Strong's Exhaustive Concordance of the Bible*. Nashville: Thomas Nelson, 1996

Warren, Rick. *The Purpose-Driven Life: What on Earth Am I Here For?* Grand Rapids: Zondervan, 2002.

Williamson, Marianne. *A Return to Love: Reflections on the Principles of* A Course in Miracles. New York: HarperPerennial, 1993.